# Holy Ghost Creek

Fishing circa 1959.

# Holy Ghost Creek

Frank D. Weissbarth

UNIVERSITY OF NEW MEXICO PRESS
ALBUQUERQUE

© 2004 by the University of New Mexico Press
All rights reserved. Published 2004
Printed and bound in the United States of America

10  09  08  07  06  05  04   1  2  3  4  5  6  7


Library of Congress Cataloging-in-Publication Data

Weissbarth, Frank D., 1947–
Holy Ghost Creek / Frank D. Weissbarth.— 1st ed.
p. cm.
Includes bibliographical references.
ISBN 0-8263-3428-8 (cloth : alk. paper)
1. Fly fishing—New Mexico—Jemez Mountains—Anecdotes.
2. Fly fishing—Sangre de Cristo Mountains (Colo. and N.M.)—Anecdotes.
3. Rivers—New Mexico. I. Title.
SH527.E45 2004
799.12´4´097895—dc22
2004005276


All photographs © Frank D. Weissbarth
Map © 2003 Michael Brown

Design and composition by Maya Allen-Gallegos
Typeset in Centaur 12.5/14
Display type set in Arcana and Centaur Family

*This is for my father,*
ARTHUR WEISSBARTH,
*who took me fishing.*

# Epigraph

We forest officers, who acquiesced in the extinguishment of the bear, knew a local rancher who had plowed up a dagger engraved with the name of one of Coronado's captains. We spoke harshly of the Spaniards who, in their zeal for gold and converts, had needlessly extinguished the native Indians. It did not occur to us that we, too, were the captains of an invasion too sure of its own righteousness.

Escudilla still hangs on the horizon, but when you see it you no longer think of bear. It's only a mountain now.

—Aldo Leopold,
*A Sand County Almanac*

# TABLE OF CONTENTS

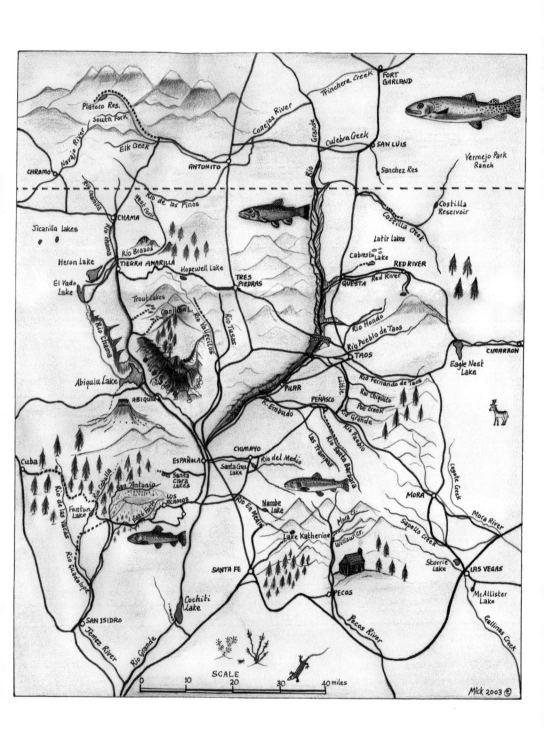

FORT GARLAND

Platoro Res.
South Fork
Navajo River
Elk Creek
CHROMO
Rio Chamita
West Fork
CHAMA
Rio de los Pinos
Rio Chama
Rio Brazos
TIERRA AMARILLA
Hopewell Lake
Heron Lake
Jicarilla Lakes
El Vado Lake
Trout Lakes
Canjilon L.
Rio Vallecitos
Rio Tusas
Abiquiu Lake
ABIQUIU

ANTONITO
Conejos River
Trinchera Creek
Rio Grande
Culebra Creek
SAN LUIS
Sanchez Res
Yermejo Park Ranch
Costilla Reservoir
Costilla Creek
Latir Lakes
Cabresto Lake
RED RIVER
QUESTA
Red River
Rio Hondo
Rio Pueblo de Taos
TRES PIEDRAS
TAOS
CIMARRON
Eagle Nest Lake
Rio Fernando de Taos
Rio Chiquito
Pot Creek
PILAR
PEÑASCO
R. Embudo
Little Rio Grande
Rio Pueblo
Rio Santa Barbara
Las Trampas
CHIMAYO
Rio del Medio
Santa Cruz Lake
ESPAÑOLA
Santa Clara Lakes
Rio Cebolla
San Antonio
East Fork
LOS ALAMOS
Rio En Medio
Nambe Lake
Lake Katherine
Mora Cr.
Willow Cr.
MORA
Coyote Creek
Mora River
Sapello Creek
Storrie Lake
LAS VEGAS
McAllister Lake
Gallinas Creek
Cuba
Rio de las Vacas
Fenton Lake
Rio Guadalupe
SANTA FE
Jemez River
SAN ISIDRO
Cochiti Lake
Rio Grande
PECOS
Pecos River

SCALE
0    10    20    30    40 miles

Mick 2003 ©

# Author's Note

One of the quandaries I faced in writing this book had to do with whether to give the names of streams. It is not as simple as it might sound. I felt a good deal of internal conflict between worries about the impact that disclosing secret streams might have on the quality of the experience I have had on these waters and a desire to be fair to readers. Much of the allure of fishing in small streams has to do with solitude. I would trade all—no, make that most—of the big trout in the world for the opportunity to fish alone.

Solitude and fine fishing can often be found together on small streams. They seldom coexist on big rivers. A friend told me that the last time he fished the San Juan, on a weekday in autumn, he was struck by the number of people on the river. He stopped fishing and counted. From the spot where he stood, he could see twenty-seven other fishermen. It was not his idea of fun, and it is not mine. I have never seen another fisherman on one of the streams described in this book. On others, meeting another fisherman is a rare occurrence.

Solitude is one thing. The quality of the fishing is another. Some of the streams described in this book are very small, and even though the fishing is often very good, the overall number of fish is limited. A greedy or destructive fisherman could do real damage to such streams over the course of a summer.

And then there is the allure of secrecy. Small stream fishermen are a breed apart. They are notoriously close-mouthed. Information about small streams is not easy to come by. That is part of the game. No one tells you much. When you fish a new stream, you never really know what you are going to find. The stream might be overgrown or it might be open. The trout might be sleek or they might be stunted. There might be pools and beaver dams or the water might cascade down the mountain in a rush. The only constant is that the stream is never what you expect. Knowledge is hard won and based mostly on personal experience. Such knowledge is seldom given away.

On the other hand, this is a book about real experiences in real places. I did not think it fair to the readers to conceal the identities of the waters described in this book. What emerged was a sort of compromise. In the essays concerning larger rivers like the Rio Grande and the Los Pinos, I included the names of the rivers. I also named smaller streams that I felt were already sufficiently well-known to the fishing public so that their inclusion in this book was not likely to result in any significant increase in fishing pressure.

There are, however, a few streams that I did not name. They are all real places, and they share certain common characteristics. They are small, largely unknown to other fishermen, and seldom fished. I like them that way, and I just could not bring myself to name them. In these instances I included sufficient information about the character of the stream and its general location to enable anyone who is really and truly interested in finding and fishing it to do so.

# INTRODUCTION

On a summer day several years ago I walked down into the Cruces Basin near the Colorado border. It was an easy hike through open woods of aspen and spruce. For much of the way, the trail followed an empty streambed. The ground was dry. The sky above the Basin was cloudless and deep blue. Halfway down I saw a grouse perched high in a tree. We watched each other for several moments. Then the grouse looked away. I continued on down the slope. After a final steep descent I entered the Basin, a great grassy meadow surrounded by green hills. The hills did not look high, but they rose to eleven thousand feet, and even in July there was snow on the ridge tops. In the meadow three tiny streams joined to form Beaver Creek, a tributary to the Rio de los Pinos, which in turn ran east to join the Rio Grande. According to the Game and Fish Department's guide to New Mexico fishing waters, Beaver Creek held brook trout. It did.

After rigging my small fly rod, I fished down the creek, beginning where it left the meadow and entered the woods. I fished sunlit riffles and shaded pools. I fished through the beaver ponds that gave the creek its name. Everywhere I caught brook trout. They were small jeweled fish, none larger than eight inches. They attacked wet flies and dries with equal abandon. I released them all, but when noon approached, I wished I had thought to bring a frying pan. Instead, I had to settle for peanut butter and jelly sandwiches and a chocolate bar.

After lunch I walked back up the stream to the meadow. The grass was tall, and grasshoppers jumped out of my way as I walked through it. I tied on a hopper pattern and began to fish up the stream. The creek flowed over a gravel bottom. In most places it was no more than six feet wide, and it was shallow enough so that I could cross it easily in my hiking boots. Here and there I came upon an undercut bank or a deeper pocket formed along the outer edge of a bend in the stream. The trout liked the hopper pattern, but it was a big fly and

1

the fish were so small that they had difficulty taking it in their mouths.

Some time after entering the meadow I came upon a shallow run where the stream flowed over a pale bottom of small stones. Hard against the opposite bank there was a slot of deeper water, perhaps a foot deep. I cast the hopper. An instant after it hit the water, a small trout hit the fly. I struck but was too slow. I cast again. The fly landed six feet farther up the stream and began its drift down the band of darker water in the afternoon sun. I tensed and waited for the strike. It came in an explosion of spray. The leader parted and a heavy trout raced upstream, leaving a broad vee-shaped wake as it fled.

It was an event so unexpected that after it occurred I could fish no longer. Oh, I did tie on another fly and catch a few more small brookies, but the big trout had taken my only hopper, and my heart was no longer in fishing. It took only a few dark clouds far to the northwest to convince me that it was time to go. On the way out of the Basin I wondered whether the big fish had been a brook trout or perhaps a brown up from the Los Pinos. Its presence in the shallow meadow stream no more than six feet wide high up in the mountains was a mystery. It remains so to this day.

Fishing is for me a microcosm of the great mystery. My earliest memories of life are as a small boy lying on the warm wood of a dock, looking down through a knothole into green water where sunfish appeared, hung suspended, and vanished like ghosts. Where they came from and where they went I did not know. It is still that way. Though I now know something of where the fish reside and how they live, the knowledge only deepens my sense of wonder. The fish never cease to confound and surprise me. The big fish in that tiny stream, the river so generous one day and barren the next, the wild trout that thrive in a trickle on the edge of town.

There are things beneath the surface of the river that I will never know. There is not time enough to learn them and the river is always changing. But sometimes, on a rare day, for a few moments or hours, the barrier between water and land vanishes and I see the trout in their watery world and hear the sound of the stream and the wind in the trees and watch as insects hover over the water and a mink slips silently along the bank. It is an intimacy born of long hours on the water, of study and of love. It is why I fish.

*Chapter One*

## The Land, the Streams, and the Trout

Northern New Mexico is a land of contrasts. Seen from the air, it is brown empty country. Here and there mountain ranges rise from the plain. Their forms are dark, and the ranges appear small. On the ground it is different. The brown empty land is made up of rolling high desert and open valleys intersected by numerous arroyos. There are few live streams. Sparse golden grasses mix with pale green chamisa and cholla cactus. The country is dotted with the low dark forms of piñons and junipers. Cottonwoods grow along the arroyos and wherever there are springs or running water.

As you make your way into the foothills, the piñons and junipers become thicker, and by the time you turn onto a dirt road into the mountains, ponderosa pines begin to appear. As the road climbs, the pines grow taller, and soon they have entirely replaced the piñons and junipers. Beneath the pines there are small stands of gambels oak. If you continue to climb, you will come upon groves of slim white aspens and green open meadows. In the summer the meadows are filled with wildflowers. Higher still, fir and spruce replace the pines, and eventually, on the tallest mountains, the trees give way to bare rocky slopes.

There are two principal mountain ranges. East of the Rio Grande the Sangre de Cristo Mountains rise to more than thirteen thousand feet. The range is the southernmost extension of the great Rocky Mountain chain that runs north from Santa Fe on up into Canada. The mountains are large, steep, and densely wooded. They are home to elk, mule deer, black bears, mountain lions, and a host of smaller creatures. Numerous streams run down out of the Sangre de Cristos.

They feed the Canadian River Drainage in the east, the Pecos in the South, and the Rio Grande in the West.

The Sangre de Cristo Mountains are far from uniform. The western edge of the range is a long series of sharp craggy peaks. As you move east, the mountains are smoother and more rounded. The difference is in the rocks. The high peaks along the western front are composed of ancient granite, quartzite, amphibolite, and schist formed in Precambrian times more than 1.5 billion years ago. These rocks are all very hard and resistant to the forces of erosion. The mountains are rough and steep, and soil forms slowly. The landscape is visually dramatic but biologically poor. The streams that descend from the western front of the Sangre de Cristos are mostly steep, swift and very clear.

In the eastern part of the range, the ancient Precambrian rocks lie beneath a thin blanket of tan Mississippian rock and a thicker layer of Pennsylvanian sediments, limestones and, shales. These rocks are softer than the Precambrian bedrock and quicker to yield to forces of water, wind, and time. The mountains they form are rounded and less steep. The soils are richer too, and game is more plentiful. The streams in the eastern part of the range are generally less turbulent than those farther west, but they still flow swiftly.

West of the Rio Grande are the Jemez Mountains. They extend some forty miles from Jemez Pueblo in the south to Coyote in the north and an equal distance from Española in the east to Cuba in the west. Seen from a distance, the Jemez looks unremarkable, a series of long rolling mountains rising up from the Rio Grande Valley. But if you look at the Jemez from the air, or on the relief map in my living room, one feature leaps out. At the heart of the range there is an enormous empty crater, some twelve miles in diameter.

The Jemez is what remains of an immense ancient volcano that was once among the dominant features of the North American landscape. Some estimates place its height at more than twenty thousand feet. A million years ago the volcano exploded in a blast whose size defies comprehension, leaving an empty crater, the caldera, a dozen miles across. The greatest volcanic explosion in recorded history was the eruption of Krakatoa in 1883. It was heard three thousand miles away. The Jemez explosion was many times larger.

After the explosion, the volcano cooled. Rains fell, and the caldera filled with water. But the volcano was not dead. Beneath the lake, the great forces that created the volcano were still at work. The floor of the lake rose and the lake spilled out over the sides of the caldera in torrents that scarred the mountains and cut deep canyons through the volcanic rock. Today the caldera is called the Valle Grande. It is a treeless grassland surrounded on all sides by forested hills and intersected with the headwaters of many streams. Cattle and elk graze there. In the vastness of the caldera, they appear no larger than insects.

If you leave the Valle Grande, you enter a land of wooded mountains cut by steep canyons created when the lake that once filled the caldera overflowed. Small streams run along the canyon floors. They flow out of the Jemez to the Chama in the north, the Rio Grande in the east and the Rio San Jose in the west. The streams are smaller than those that descend from the Sangre de Cristos, and they flow more gently. Wildlife abounds. There are flowers in the clearings. As you walk along a wooded trail in the Jemez, it is sometimes hard to believe that you are in the heart of a volcano. But if you look more closely, the evidence is everywhere in the rocks around you. The pale rock on the high ridges is tuff composed of volcanic ash. The dark rock along the canyon floor is basalt, cooled lava.

New Mexico is very dry. It receives less precipitation than all but two of the other fifty states. Ninety-seven percent of the water that enters the state in flowing streams, rain, and snow is lost through evaporation. Despite the dryness of the surrounding country, both the Sangre de Cristos and the Jemez receive ample precipitation. In most years the mountains are blanketed by snow in the winter and are magnets for thunderstorms in July and August.

New Mexico is also high country. In the northern part of the state, altitudes range from 5,500 feet in the valleys to nearly 12,000 feet in the Jemez and more than 13,000 feet in the Sangre de Cristos. The "lowlands" are comparatively warm and dry but as you move up into the mountains, the climate grows progressively cooler and wetter. In the Pecos Wilderness, summertime temperatures average around seventy degrees, annual precipitation is thirty-five to forty inches and snow has been reported in every month of the year except July.

New Mexico is a land of edges. It is on the western edge of the Great Plains and on the southern edge of the Rocky Mountains and the Colorado Plateau. It is on the southeastern edge of the basin and range country and forms the northern edge of the Sonoran Desert. Within New Mexico's boundaries are found six of the seven life zones ranging from Arctic Alpine to lower Sonoran. Because of the wide variety of habitats, the state is home to a diverse and extensive assembly of fish and game. But because many native species, including trout, are found here at the peripheries of their range, they are extremely vulnerable to environmental degradation and serve as sensitive indicators of the health of ecosystems.

When fly fishermen across the country think of New Mexico, they think of the fabled fishing for big rainbows on the San Juan River in the northwest corner of the state. A really knowledgeable angler might know about the fall fishing for brown trout in the Rio Grande Gorge or about the browns and rainbows in the Chama below El Vado dam. Three rivers. About what you would expect in a desert state, but there is more—much more. Those big rivers are all fine places to fish, but they are only a small fraction of what New Mexico has to offer.

The state's real wealth is in its small streams. There are two reasons for this. The first is that there are several hundred small streams in the mountains of northern New Mexico that hold trout. Most contain good populations of wild fish. The second is that almost all of these streams are located within the confines of the Santa Fe and Carson National Forests, so they are accessible to the public. Accessible, however, does not necessarily mean easy to reach. While a few streams are followed by paved roads, many others require a long ride down a dirt forest road and still more can only be reached by trail. As a general rule, the farther you have to walk to reach a stream, the better the fishing. Altitudes range from 7,000 feet to 10,000 feet and more, and the weather can be unpredictable. Fishing hike-in streams requires preparation and common sense.

It is hard to generalize about the streams. There are a lot of them and each is unique. Some spill down boulder-strewn mountainsides. Others meander through grassy open meadows. Some sparkle in sunlight. Others run in perpetual shade beneath a canopy of trees. The trees along the bank might be sweet-smelling cottonwoods, dense willows, tall ponderosa pines, douglas firs, or slim white aspens. The water might be rich and fertile or it might be comparatively barren. The trout might be many or few. They might be thin and stunted or sleek and fat. When you fish a new stream, you never know what you will find.

Nothing is static. Even familiar waters change. The beaver pond that seems so placid and timeless as you cast through the willows to the place where circles spread on the still dark water might be gone in the spring, leaving only an empty mud flat, a broken barrier of sticks along the scoured streambed, or no trace at all except in your memory. The deep overhung run against the far bank where caddis flies dance above the water and vanish in small splashy rises might not be there the next time you fish the creek. Streams are forever moving and changing and cutting new channels. Nothing stays the same.

Still, the streams that run out of the mountains have many things in common. They are almost all small or very small streams. New Mexico's Game and Fish Department defines a small stream as one whose flow is normally less than fifteen cubic feet per second. I use a more functional definition. If I can comfortably fish a stream in hiking boots without feeling a need to wade it, then it is a small stream. At the large end of the spectrum are streams like the Santa Barbara and Elk Creek above Second Meadows where my hiking boots are usually soaked after a few hours of fishing. The small end of the spectrum is harder to define, and I haven't found it yet. But I'm trying.

Several years ago while driving along a dirt road in the Jemez, I crossed what looked like an overgrown ditch running through a small meadow of knee-high grass. On a whim I stopped and took a look. The "ditch" was no more than a couple of feet across, but the water was deep and clear. When I approached, a pair of foot-long trout raced upstream into the shade where the tiny stream emerged from a tangle of willows.

The streams have another characteristic in common. They are all cold water streams. The waters that descend from the Sangre de Cristo and Jemez range from cold to icy, depending on the altitude and the season. They are almost always clear except at the peak of spring runoff when melting snow may cloud them or after a particularly heavy summer rain. Trout are creatures of cold clear waters, so it should come as no surprise that trout are found in virtually every stream in the Sangre de Cristo and Jemez Mountains.

Before the Spanish came to New Mexico, the state's waters held four kinds of native trout. There were Rio Grande cutthroats in the Rio Grande, Pecos, and Canadian drainages. There were Colorado cutthroats in the San Juan River and its tributaries. There were Gila trout in the Gila River watershed. And there was an unnamed trout that inhabited the Mimbres River in southern New Mexico. Today, only the Rio Grande cutthroat survives in fishable populations.

Originally all the waters suitable for trout in the Rio Grande, Pecos, and Canadian River drainages held Rio Grande cutthroat trout. They are the southernmost members of the far-flung cutthroat clan, and they live near the southern edge of trout country. Their ancestors originally swam in the coastal waters of the Pacific Northwest. They moved to the rivers to spawn and the ocean to feed. Coastal cutthroats still populate the rivers and estuaries from northern California to Alaska.

The precise routes by which cutthroat trout reached New Mexico remain a mystery. What is known is that during the ice ages ancestral cutthroat trout followed rivers inland to the feet of the great glaciers that extended south into the Sangre de Cristos. During interglacial periods, they crossed the Rockies and penetrated south and east, eventually reaching the Rio Grande, Pecos, and Canadian River drainages.

During glacial times, from about 130,000 to 10,000 years ago, great lakes filled the basins of the Southwest. For the cutthroat trout, the lakes were miniature freshwater versions of the oceans in which their ancestors swam. Time passed. The climate grew drier. The lakes shrank. Today, with a few exceptions, such as Pyramid Lake in Nevada, they are gone.

As the waters receded, the connecting waterways vanished and populations of cutthroat trout were isolated. Isolation in differing habitats led to the development of distinct subspecies of cutthroat trout. They ranged from small colorful stream fish like the greenback cutthroat of Colorado to big silvery lake fish like the lahontan cutthroats of Pyramid Lake that once averaged more than twenty pounds and supported a commercial fishery. Interior cutthroats may have many spots like the fine-spotted Snake River cutthroats or comparatively few like the Yellowstone cutthroats. The cutthroats that reached the waters of northern New Mexico evolved into deep-bodied colorful fish with large, irregularly shaped black spots clustered toward their tails and distinct red cutthroat slash marks beneath their gill covers. These fish are known by the scientific name of *Onchoryncchus clarki virginalis.* We call them Rio Grande cutthroat trout.

Biologists agree that Rio Grande cutthroats have been extirpated from over 90 percent of their historic range, but considerable controversy exists about how many populations of Rio Grande cutthroats remain in New Mexico and southern Colorado. The numbers range from 106 populations in New Mexico and 161 in Colorado down to a total of less than 70. The main reason for the discrepancy is that many populations are hybridized to one degree or another with the rainbow trout. The numbers at the high end of the range include these hybrid populations. The numbers at the low end don't. As a result, they more accurately reflect the condition of the subspecies. Even at the low end, however, the numbers are deceiving. Most of the streams are tiny, and the numbers of fish they hold are commensurately small, sometimes no more than a few hundred individuals.

They do not fare well in competition with the brown, rainbow, or brook trout, and they are among the easiest trout to catch. The introduction of brown, rainbow, and brook trout coupled with declines in water quality and quantity caused by livestock grazing, agriculture, mining, and logging have eliminated Rio Grande cutthroats from many waters. Rio Grande cutthroats no longer exist in any of the main rivers. In absolute terms, the number of Rio Grande cutthroats is small. Both New Mexico and Colorado have programs aimed at protecting Rio Grande cutthroats and expanding their range. Until recently, these programs focused on tiny isolated stream segments, but in 2002, the New Mexico Game and Fish Department began a number of projects aimed at restoring "meta-populations" of native trout to larger watersheds. While restoration efforts have met with some success, the forces that have eliminated Rio Grande cutthroats from more than 90 percent of their historic range continue unabated, and their future is far from assured.

Rio Grande cutthroats were not the only native trout in New Mexico. In the northwest corner of the state, there were Colorado cutthroats. These fish are rare in Colorado and were thought to be extinct in New Mexico. Several years ago, however, Mike Hatch at the Game and Fish Department told me that an inbred remnant population had been found in a stream in the Chuska Mountains. He did not volunteer the name of the stream and I did not ask.

In the Gila National Forest in southwestern New Mexico, there are a handful of streams that hold Gila trout. They are found here and in southeastern Arizona and nowhere else in the world. The Gila trout is a federally listed endangered species. Gila trout face the same threats as Rio Grande cutthroats: predation by stocked brown trout, hybridization with stocked rainbows, and declines in water quality and quantity caused by unsound grazing and logging practices. But Gila trout face other threats as well. Some residents of Catron and Grant counties resent the fish because they see their federally endangered status as a threat to historic grazing and logging practices. And the fact that Gila trout are found in only a few streams in a relatively small geographical region places the species at risk when wildfires rage in the Gila National Forest, as they have on several occasions in recent years.

The continued existence of Gila trout is due to thirty years of work by game and fish officers in an often hostile setting. In recent years their efforts have begun to bear fruit. Gila trout have been reintroduced in a number of streams and a major restoration project is under way on the upper West Fork of the Gila. As a result, the Gila trout may soon be "downlisted" from endangered to threatened. However, unless local attitudes toward the fish change and further steps are taken to protect their habitat and expand their range, the prognosis for their survival can at best be described as guarded.

Finally, there is—or was—the trout of the Mimbres River. The Mimbres is a small river that drains the slopes of the Black Range in southern New Mexico before flowing into Mexico where it ends in the Guzman Basin. In 1846, a young army lieutenant named William H. Emory was assigned to perform a reconnaissance to assess the value of the lands that the United States was bent on taking by force from Mexico. Emory wrote a detailed summary of his daily observations, describing the peoples he met, the terrain, the availability of water, and the flora and fauna he encountered. He was a keen and educated observer. When he reached the Mimbres River on October 17, 1846, he wrote:

> [I]ts valley was truly beautiful, about one mile wide, of rich fertile soil, densely covered with cotton-wood, walnut, ash, &c. It is a rapid, dashing stream, about fifteen feet wide and three deep, affording sufficient water to irrigate its beautiful valley. It is filled with trout. (Emory, 96–7)

With what trout we will never know. Like many streams in New Mexico, the Mimbres no longer carries the volume of water it held a century and a half ago. There are still trout in the upper Mimbres, but they are stocked rainbows and browns or their descendants. The native trout of the Mimbres River no longer exists. We can surmise that it belonged to a species or subspecies separate and apart from New Mexico's other native trout because the Guzman Basin is a closed basin that is not connected to any of the watersheds in which those other trout live. We can only wonder at what manner of trout it may have been.

Today the Rio Grande Cutthroat is the only native trout that survives in fishable populations in the streams of northern New Mexico. Most of the fishing is for other trout species. Beginning shortly before the turn of the last century, brown, rainbow and, to a lesser degree, brook trout were stocked in streams throughout the state. As in other places, the men who stocked the trout did so with an almost messianic zeal. They stocked streams so small they hardly seemed worth the trouble. They stocked streams so difficult to reach that they literally risked their lives in the process. They stocked every stream they could reach.

The end result of all that stocking is a decidedly mixed bag. Brown trout took hold in many places, and there are now numerous self-sustaining populations. In most streams the State has not stocked brown trout for many years. Any brown trout that you catch today is almost certainly a wild, stream-bred fish. Wild rainbows are found in a number of streams, but for the most part, the rainbow trout fishery remains a put-and-take proposition. There are brook trout in a handful of streams, but in most places where they occur, the fish are stunted. All of these trout fill ecological niches once inhabited by Rio Grande cutthroats. In the main rivers, the Chama, Pecos and Rio Grande, no native trout remain. The cutthroats that hang on in the headwaters are only a shadow of what once was.

The brown trout in New Mexico are like brown trout everywhere. They are cautious, wary fish and more tolerant of warm or turbid waters than other species. Their appearance varies widely from stream to stream. In some places, they are deep butter yellow or almost orange. In others, they are almost silvery with only a faint brownish tinge. The black spots that cover their backs and the white spots with red centers that line their sides might be many and fine or large and comparatively few. Browns have the deserved reputation of being finicky eaters and the undeserved reputation of being poor fighters. In the nutrient-poor mountain streams of New Mexico, however, brown trout cannot afford to be selective except during the height of infrequent hatches. They will rise freely to almost any well presented dry fly. When they take, they fight strongly and well.

Rainbow trout are the easiest trout to raise in hatcheries. They grow quickly and over the years strains have been developed that are well adapted to life in open hatchery raceways. They are dumped by the thousands into New Mexico streams. Hatchery rainbows are dumb, sluggish, and often misshapen. The wild fish are another story. They are sleek black-spotted trout with a broad pink or reddish stripe that runs laterally along their sides. Wild rainbows are strong and athletic fish, and in a proper setting, a flat meadow stream with ample food and shelter, wild rainbows can be as maddeningly selective as the most educated brown trout.

Brook trout are among my favorite fish. They are among the most beautiful of trout, dark and spotted yellow, red, and white, with bright orange fins edged in black and white. Like the native cutthroats, they are intolerant of warm or polluted waters. And like cutthroats, they are gullible and more easily caught than brown or rainbow trout.

In his book, *Beatty's Cabin* (1953), Elliot Barker, New Mexico's first game warden, described his adventures hunting and fishing in the

Pecos high country in the early years of the twentieth century. He wrote of red-bellied native trout and hundred-fish days. Those days are gone. And yet, despite all the changes, the fishing, at least in the eyes of this transplanted Easterner, remains superb. Once you get away from the road, the streams are filled with trout. The trout are not large, but in many streams they are large enough. The trout may not be natives, but most of the fish you see will be wild. The trout are not selective. They will strike at almost any small dry fly, but if you make a sloppy cast or fail to respect their natural caution as you approach, you will never know they are there.

Solitude is only a short hike down a river. The mountain streams of northern New Mexico remain places where you can fish all day and not see another angler. Rocky canyon walls and dark firs tower above you. Aspen leaves shimmer in the wind. There are flowers in the meadow. Small white clouds float by in an endless sky of blue. In early afternoon the clouds darken and grow. Thunder rocks the mountains. Lightning crashes and rain falls. Then the storm recedes, and by early evening when caddis flies dance above the darkening riffles, the sky is as empty and clear as it was when the day began. So now, the stage has been set. It's time to go fishing.

# Chapter Two

# HOLY GHOST CREEK

oly Ghost Creek is a tiny brook, little more than a trickle. It is one of several such streams that rise high in the Sangre de Cristo Mountains east of Santa Fe and join to form the Pecos River in the southernmost valley of the Rocky Mountains. In a well-watered place such a stream would not be noticed. It might not have a name. Northern New Mexico is a dry land. While the Sangre de Cristos receive heavy snow in winter and frequent thunderstorms in summer, they are surrounded by high desert on the west and south and arid plains to the east. Any stream that carries water the year around is important here. Holy Ghost Creek has a name and appears on every map.

From its confluence with the Pecos at Terrero to the National Forest campground three miles upstream, the creek runs through a densely wooded canyon. Tall ponderosa pines and douglas firs shade the stream and the summer homes along its banks. At the campground the canyon opens into a steep valley. Aspens begin to mix with the pines, and willows grow along the creek. The campground is large and usually crowded. Between Memorial Day and Labor Day it is a place to be avoided, but the road ends there so it is the starting place for my walks.

The state of New Mexico stocks rainbow trout in Holy Ghost Creek. The little stream is heavily fished during the spring and summer months. Salmon eggs and worms are drifted through every pocket and pool. Few, if any, of the stocked rainbows survive long enough to drift down to the Pecos. By the time summer officially ends, the campground is empty and the rainbows are gone.

Fall arrives. The skies are clear and endless and impossibly blue. The leaves on the aspens are bright yellow. The stream is low and clear. The parking lot at the campground is empty except for the occasional hiker's car. The brown trout appear in Holy Ghost Creek.

Some have undoubtedly come up from the Pecos to spawn, but most have been in the little stream all along. How they survive the hordes of summer fishermen is something of a mystery, but there are clues. Salmon eggs are the bait of choice along the Pecos and its tributaries. Rainbow trout love salmon eggs, a genetic legacy of their development in the streams of the Pacific Northwest. Brown trout are indifferent to salmon eggs. They much prefer to eat the insects that live in and near the creek.

Most of the rainbows in Holy Ghost Creek grew up in the open raceways of Lisboa Springs Hatchery a few miles down the Pecos. They are used to plenty of human company. Brown trout are by nature shy fish, and the state of New Mexico has not stocked them in Holy Ghost Creek for many years. The browns in the stream have all been born and bred there. In such small and shallow water a fish that is slow to sense and flee from any potential danger will not survive long. A clumsy step along the bank or a fleeting shadow may not spook the hatchery rainbows, but it will send the browns dashing for cover. The brown trout in Holy Ghost Creek are cautious fish. They are survivors.

Neither brown trout nor rainbows are native to the Pecos drainage. Originally the streams held only Rio Grande cutthroats. They are lovely fish but relatively easy to catch. New Mexico has always had generous bag limits. Too generous. As access improved and population grew, streams were degraded by logging, agriculture, and cattle. Fishing pressure increased, and the number of cutthroats declined. Rainbow trout from the West Coast and brown trout from Europe were stocked in the streams to bolster the fishing. Rainbows hybridize with cutthroats, and both rainbows and browns are more aggressive than the native trout. They drive the cutthroats from the best feeding stations and lies into marginal water where survival is uncertain. The introduction of these foreign fish, however well intended, hastened the demise of the Rio Grande cutthroat in the Pecos watershed.

Brown trout are now firmly established in Holy Ghost Creek. They are born, live out their lives, and die in the stream. Rainbows are interlopers, temporary sacrificial offerings placed in the creek for the pleasure of summer fishermen. They are ill-equipped for survival, and their lives in the wild are perilous and short. No one has studied the interaction between brown and rainbow trout in Holy Ghost Creek. Studies of other streams suggest that the stocking of hatchery trout in a stream with a self-sustaining trout population is generally a poor idea. Here, however, the issue is complicated by easy access, the presence of the campground, and anachronistic bag limits. While the introduction of large numbers of relatively large "catchable" rainbow trout may stress the browns by creating competition for scarce food and shelter, the rainbows also serve as a buffer between the brown trout and the onslaught of summer fishermen. If rainbows were not in the stream, anglers would focus their attention on the browns with who knows what result.

The survival of the brown trout in Holy Ghost Creek is something of a miracle. As I walk along the stream on a clear fall day each trout I see appears as evidence of the triumphant resilience of nature. But appearance is not reality. Nature, in the form of the Rio Grande cutthroat, is gone from these waters. The brown trout in the stream are foreigners just like the stocked rainbows. They are here because men brought them here from another continent five thousand miles away, and the native trout are gone, at least in part because of their presence. Unlike the rainbows, however, the brown trout are tenacious, adaptable, and wild. Given half a chance, they will be here long after I am gone. That knowledge sustains me.

\* \* \*

## OCTOBER 29, 1989

It was the first day when you could really feel winter. The sky was cloudless and deep blue, and the sun was strong. But in the shade of the trees the air was cold, and the wind was raw. The creek ran low and clear through the empty campground. I spotted an occasional trout in the deeper pockets and thought I saw shadows in the runs. Danny and I made our way past the end of the campground and crossed a small bridge over the stream. Danny picked up one stick after another. "Swords," he called them. He fought imaginary battles with bushes and stands of tall grass that grew near the creek. The sticks served as fishing rods too, and they were pretty handy for stirring mud at the edge of the water.

Then Danny found some tall grass with big heads of seeds. He picked one and told me it was a "cattail" that he had picked for mommy. A few moments later the cattail was gone, replaced by another stick.

Less than two hundred yards above the campground we came to a place where fresh beaver cuttings were everywhere. In addition to willows, the beavers had cut down a big aspen more than a foot in diameter. I showed Danny the stump and the fallen tree and white wood chips on the ground. I told him how the beavers had cut down the tree with their teeth. He asked if he could see one, but there were none around. I told him that they probably worked at night.

There was a series of dams. Each one held trout. The shadows of the fish glided like dark ghosts over the light silt bottom. They were brown trout and incredibly spooky. Whenever we made a sudden move or approach too close they would head for cover and disappear. In one of the dams I saw two really big trout, fish in the two-pound class. I wondered what they were doing here in a stream that you could literally step across in hiking boots. But before I could approach close enough to attempt to shoot a cast through a hole in the willows the two trout sensed me and were gone.

We walked up to the next dam. There was a little grassy clearing there, and we sat down and ate crackers and cheese, apples and cookies. I sat on a rock and enjoyed the sun. Danny played with a stick by the edge of the water. There was ice along the edge of the pool. Danny broke off a piece with his stick and brought it to me. "What's this?" he asked. "Ice," I told him. "Will it be winter tomorrow, Daddy?" he wanted to know. "Not tomorrow," I told him, but soon enough, I thought.

Then Danny announced that he was tired and wanted me to carry him. I put him in the pack and headed back along the trail toward the car. Danny's tired weight felt heavy in the pack. This would be the last year I would carry him when we went for walks in the woods. By the time we got back to the car the shadows were getting long, and the wind was blowing harder.

That night I dreamed about Holy Ghost Creek. My casts threaded through the willows, and the little black ant landed softly on glassy glides. Trout rose slowly to the fly. Their noses broke the surface as they inhaled it. But even in dreams I never did find a way to horse those two big trout out of the flooded willows behind the beaver dam. In the morning when I awoke the thermometer outside my window read eighteen degrees.

\* \* \*

## OCTOBER 31, 1989

Two days later I returned to the Creek in mid-afternoon after work-ing hard at my desk all morning. This time I was alone. There was more ice on the stream. The campground was deserted. As I approached the beaver ponds I could see that the beavers had been working hard. Another big aspen tree had been cut down, and wood chips were everywhere.

The ponds were freezing over. The pond where I had seen the two big trout was almost completely covered with ice. At the head of the next pond there was a run where the water was open. In the run were two nice fish. The lower fish was dark. The fish above was lighter. I tried for the lower fish first.

After hanging a back cast in the willows, I managed to get off a good cast. The little black ant landed three feet above the lower trout. I lost the fly on the broken surface immediately. The trout turned and slowly drifted downstream. Then the fish turned and headed back toward his spot. "He's lost interest," I thought. As I began to pick up the line to make another cast I felt resistance, and the trout shot toward the head of the run. The fish quickly tired and I slid it across the skin of ice at the water's edge and onto the bank.

The fish was a male brown trout a little more than a foot long with a big head and long dark body. I unhooked him and gently returned him to the stream. He swam slowly at first, gained strength and then resumed his place at the head of the run. Near him the other fish, perhaps his mate, loomed as a pale shadow. I watched for a while but did not fish. Then I walked up the creek past the other beaver dams. When the string of dams ended, Holy Ghost Creek became a tiny mountain stream again.

I followed the creek for another half-hour or so. Almost every pool held several brown trout. Most were small. The fish darted from my footsteps and my shadow. The creek was bordered by willows and small meadows of dry grass. In many places the water was shaded by the willows or the tall ponderosa pines that grew on the slopes that rose steeply from the creek. There was deer sign along the trail. The woods were empty and still. There was no wind.

The shadows were getting long, and the air was cooling rapidly. I wanted to go on, but I had promised to be home for dinner, and it was time to turn around. On the way back to the car I encountered a couple walking four large dogs. One was a white wolf hybrid. He was a magnificent animal with long powerful limbs. He moved easily through the woods with silent loping strides. The movements seemed slow and effortless, but they covered ground fast. The three dogs churned and strained as they ran, snapping twigs and generally making a racket. The wolf-dog never made a sound. He approached. Our eyes locked, his expressionless and blue. They were not the eyes of a dog. He viewed me dispassionately. Then he turned and silently disappeared through the willows.

When I was sure he was gone I turned and walked quickly down the creek towards the car in the deepening shadows. It was nearly dark by the time I got back to the campground. I did not relax until I closed the car door.

\* \* \*

## JULY 14, 1990

Every day for nearly two weeks a black mass of clouds had built up by noon over the Sangre de Cristos and late afternoon thunderstorms had rocked the mountains and Santa Fe. When I arose at 5:30 in the morning the sky was a luminous red-orange and filled with clouds. The pattern would continue. There would be more rain today.

I had been having a hard time at the office, and it had been a week of deadlines, disappointment, and moral ambivalence. The strain was beginning to tell. Sleep eluded me. I had some hard choices to make. But for now I needed badly to get away, to get some perspective and clarity. So I dressed in darkness, put my rod in the car and drove to the creek.

The campground was still asleep when I reached it. Every campsite was filled, and there were tents on the hillsides above the turnaround where I parked the car. But just a hundred yards down the trail it was a different world. Mist rose to the clouds from the tops of tall pines. The rain had washed the trail clean of footprints. Lush thigh-high grass lined the trail, wet from the night's rain. Cobwebs glistened. After a few minutes of walking my legs were soaked.

The trail ran through small meadows. Flowers were everywhere. Indian paintbrush, blue flax, purple asters, black-eyed susans, mallows, clover, and big yellow daisies. Yellow was the dominant color against the green background, but there were reds and purples and blues and whites, all muted by the clouds and mist. The only sounds were the music of the rushing stream and my footfalls on the trail.

After all the rain I had expected the creek to be high, but it was not. The winter snowpack had been low, and the rains had followed months of drought. The streams of the Sangre de Cristos are driven by snowmelt. Even after the heavy rains of the previous night, the water was gin clear. In sharp contrast to many places in the national forests of the West, there is no logging in the Holy Ghost watershed, and cattle do not graze here. The dense streamside vegetation and heavy forest cover soak up the runoff like a sponge. Despite the weeks of rain, the water was cold and clear, and the creek was in good shape.

I had intended to bypass the string of beaver ponds near the campground so that I could spend more time exploring upstream, but the sight of the mist rising from the deep, still, willow-choked water above the first dam turned my resolve to mush. In the weeks since my last visit to the creek, the beavers had cleared all the brush on my side of the pond to use in building their dam so it was possible to stand well away from the bank and still reach the water.

After dousing the little Adams dry with floatant, I cast. The fly sailed across twenty feet of land and twenty more of water before landing in deep flat water at the edge of the willows. It floated slowly on the dark mirrored surface. I watched the fly in silence. The water by the willows was deep and fishy, but I had fished here before and knew that the trout held in the broken water where the stream cascaded into the beaver pond, not here.

Suddenly the fly disappeared in a silver roll of water and the fish was on, bulldogging toward a tangle of drowned willows. The trout was small, and I turned it before it could reach the willows. A moment later it was in my hand. I released it quickly. It hovered in the thin water by my feet. Then it shot into the dark water at the base of the willows and was gone. A tiny cloud of silt was all that remained. Seconds later, that too had vanished.

The trout was an omen. Not enough of an omen to enable me to thread a cast through the willows and beneath an overhanging branch at the head of the pond to the good fish I saw rising there, but an omen nonetheless.

This spot defies me. Water spills over a small beaver dam and into the larger pond below. There is almost always a large trout resting there. The spot looks open but it is not. Willows screen the water from all directions. The fact that it is close to the head of the trail only complicates matters. I am still impatient when I get here. I want to fish, cast flies on the water, not plan strategy, but the place calls for deliberation, not action. One day when I am older I will have the wisdom to fish this place properly, I tell myself, but for now I just cast. The willows reach out to grab my fly which seldom reaches the water. The fish are happy.

On this day I was luckier than usual. My fly made it through the willows, dropped gently toward the water, . . . and landed in an overhanging branch, inches above the surface. By the time I shook it free, the big trout was gone. One day when I am older . . .

The day was windless, and the clouds and mist hid my shadow from the water. I fished out the three remaining dams quietly and carefully, moving slowly and keeping well away from the water. Each yielded a trout. The fish were small and brightly colored. They came quickly to the fly. I released them all. At the base of the last beaver dam little trout hovered and darted in the shallow flowing water. The water was clear as air. Mist rose. For a moment there was no clear line between us. The fish seemed to float, suspended in space. The rush of the stream filled my ears. Birds sang.

Above the beaver dams the stream ran through flower-filled meadows. Almost every pocket and pool held a trout. Whenever the fly lighted on the surface and floated without drag for a second or two, a trout took it. The fish rose slowly and inhaled the little dry fly with confidence. There was no need to set the hook. The deception was complete.

As I approached a slow shallow pool, the sun broke through the clouds throwing my shadow across the surface of the pool. A fine fish, better than any I had taken so far, streaked for cover. I stood motionless and watched the water, but the trout did not return. I moved on. Twenty minutes later, a foot-long brown came boiling out of a deep forested pocket to nail the Adams. The fish darted around the pocket, thrashed on the surface and then tired. I lifted him to the high rocky bank on which I stood. This one went in the creel. Dinner.

By the time the trail veered up away from the stream, I had lost count of the number of trout I had released. I followed the stream up through the woods. There was heavy brush here and no trail. The stream was tiny now. I was fishing well, sneaking up beneath every likely-looking pocket and dropping the Adams on the surface. I took two more small browns. Then I hung the fly in a tree where I could not reach it. It was the first fly I had lost all day.

I knotted on a Royal Wulff tied downwing style—red body, white wing, and a mottled brown tail. The fly resembled nothing in nature. Much has been written in attempts to explain the appeal that this fly and its progenitor, the Royal Coachman, have for trout. I have heard the flies described as everything from beetle imitations to strawberry sundaes. None of the explanations make sense. All I know for certain is that they work. Minutes later, a deep-bodied female brown trout slid slowly up from beneath an undercut bank to engulf the fly. She was as long as the dinner fish but twice as heavy. A worm hung from her mouth. I removed the fly from her lip and released her gently back into the stream.

In the next pocket a tiny trout, no more than three inches long, rose through the clear water and tried mightily to impale itself on the hook. The effort was unsuccessful, but the fish drowned the fly. The woods were too dense for false casting, so I dried the fly on my tee shirt, doused it with floatant and moved on.

Fifty yards farther up, a tree had fallen diagonally across the stream. I flipped the fly upstream. For a moment it floated along the deeper water that piled up against the fallen tree. Suddenly it disappeared. I set the hook and felt a heavy throbbing weight. The fish rushed beneath the branches, and the line went dead. The leader was snagged on a rock or branch. Was the trout still on? I gave slack. The line came alive. The fish had worked himself free of the obstruction. Moments later he was on the bank, the best fish of the day, a thirteen-inch male brown trout, potbellied and heavy. I released him. He hovered in the shallow water at my feet, gathering strength. Then he glided beneath the dark refuge of the fallen tree and was gone.

On the next cast I hung my fly in a tree and lost it. It was another omen, although it took me a while and another lost fly to realize it. The sun was starting to hit the water, and the fishing slowed. I fished a while longer and then turned back. It was 9:45 a.m.

Making my way through the woods, my feet and legs were soaked by the wet brush and tall grass. Even here, beneath the pines, there were flowers, orange and black lilies. Beside the stream a rotten log riddled by termites had been ripped apart by a bear in search of a meal. My shadow on the water sent a trout darting for the safety of an undercut bank.

When I reached the trail I started walking in earnest. The trail led back through the flower-filled meadows now brilliant in the sunlight. The sky was deep blue and filled with huge billowing cumulus clouds. Tall aspen trees with silvery white trunks grew on the hillside at the meadow's edge. The only tracks in the wet black earth of the trail were mine and those of a deer that had followed me up the path.

Halfway to the campground I met the first people I had seen all morning, two men with spinning rods and salmon eggs. They told me that they had not been doing too well and asked about the fishing further up the trail. My response was unintelligible. One of the men asked if the fish in the stream had any size. From the tone of his question it was clear that he thought he already knew the answer. I shrugged. He took it as confirmation of what he already believed.

When I reached the car there was a chocolate bar in the glove compartment. The car was in the shade of a great pine, and the chocolate had not melted. I felt great.

# Chapter Three

# The Day of the Hummingbirds

It was 1985, our first summer in New Mexico. On a Friday evening in July, my wife Randy, five-year-old son Adam, and I piled our camping gear into our old Oldsmobile station wagon and headed north. We had gotten a late start, and it was dark by the time we reached Ojo Caliente, a deep blackness that was a shock after a lifetime in the humid air of the East. Stars surrounded us as we climbed up the mesa between the black-etched forms of the piñons that lined the road. They were the only lights until we reached Tres Piedras. A yellow blinking light across the road marked the tiny hamlet, and then we were into the night again.

Just before reaching Antonito we turned west onto a rough and narrow road. It was night and we could not see what the country was like. We followed the road into a small village. Consulting the map, we realized that we had missed a turnoff and were in San Miguel. We retraced our path, found the road and continued west. Soon we reached the Los Pinos. The road was dirt now, and it followed close by the little river. We drove by some campsites but nothing that moved us. Adam was wide awake in the back seat.

The road grew rougher and finally I pulled over into a small grassy area beneath some old cottonwoods. We were all dead tired. The prospect of pitching the tent in the dark was not appealing, especially since we could not tell if this was a spot where we would want to make camp, so we decided to sleep in the station wagon. Adam was excited by the prospect of sleeping in the car. To him it was a great adventure. Minutes after we had folded down the back seat and spread our sleeping bags in the back of the station wagon, Randy and Adam were asleep.

The back of the station wagon was hot and stuffy, and I had a hard time falling asleep. I listened to the slow breathing of my wife and son, the chirping of crickets, and the sound of the river. I woke early. Randy and Adam were still sound asleep. I got out of the car as quietly as I could and went to the river. It was a clear stream, neither small nor large, running over a rocky bottom. The water sluiced through a narrow run and up against a rocky wall before trailing out into a shallow pool. On the other side of the Los Pinos, above the rock wall, there were dark rolling hills covered with the pines that gave the river its name. On our side of the river, the hills were bare with only sparse grasses, sagebrush and an occasional piñon. In places they broke away into jagged cliffs of pink rock.

It was cold so I took the stove from the car and made some coffee. Then I sat down to drink it on the bank of the river as the light made its way down the pine-covered hills toward the river as the sun rose. Steam curled from the cup in my hand. I watched the moving surface and listened to the sound of the water. Sunlight fell on the pool, illuminating the water. A trout rose. A moment later it rose again. Soon it was joined by another. I looked for insects on the surface but saw nothing. In a matter of minutes trout were rising throughout the pool, and I could see them flashing after nymphs in the riffle at its head.

Then I looked downstream. It seemed as though glistening clouds of snow hung suspended in the sunlight above the surface of the river as far downstream as I could see. The clouds rose and fell as if alive. Small dark forms darted through the clouds, hung suspended and then flashed away. It took me a while to realize what I was seeing. The clouds were composed of millions of tiny mayflies, their wings shimmering in the sunlight. The dark forms were hummingbirds. They would dart into the cloud of insects, take a few while suspended in midair, and then race into the shelter of the trees and streamside brush.

My wife and son joined me. We set up folding chairs on the bank of the stream and ate breakfast as we watched the show. Hummingbirds fed only on nectar, at least that was what I had always read and observed, but here, amid swarms of tiny shimmering insects, they made use of the rich food supply that filled the air.

After finishing his cereal Adam sat on my lap. At five, he was just reaching the point in his life where memory and experience made life intelligible and borders emerged between the fantastic and the routine. Was the scene we were witnessing special to him or was it simply one more new experience in a world where each observation was still unique? I could not tell. But for a long while he sat very still on my lap and watched the birds and insects.

As the sun rose higher and the morning warmed, large gray mayflies began to appear on the surface of the stream. They floated in the current with their wings held high like little sailboats. Trout were rising everywhere. I counted nearly twenty fish in the pool. Some looked quite respectable. When I could stand it no longer, I went to the car, got my small fly rod, tied on a size 12 Adams and began to fish. Trout rose with abandon. In the head of the pool, I caught a half-dozen fish without moving. I gave Adam the rod so that he could bring in the fish. We released them all. Then I moved up the stream and fished alone. In the next two hours I caught more than forty trout. A handful of the fish were hatchery rainbows but most were wild browns from ten to twelve inches. Several were larger.

I waded wet in shorts and wading shoes. The water was very cold and in places the banks were overgrown with willows. But on days like this you do not feel the cold and the willows do not reach out to grab your flies as you cast. I worked my way up the stream catching trout after trout. After a time I reached a two-foot deep run where the river flowed quickly over a rocky bottom. Near the bank, almost directly upstream, there was a boulder. In the lee of the boulder there was a quiet pocket. It looked like a place where a fish should be, so I watched the still water. Nothing rose. Then I heard a splash. Ripples spread from the unseen water above the boulder. A moment later there was another splash. Again the ripples spread.

I cast my fly directly over the boulder into the hidden water above it. The leader draped over the rock and I could not see the fly. Then I heard a splash and I set the hook. A heavy fish ran into the current, held still, then bulldogged upstream. A few moments later the trout, a seventeen-inch brown lay in the shallows. After admiring the fish I released it and watched it swim slowly up along the edge of the stream, gathering strength before darting into deeper water.

On the way back to the campsite, I caught three foot-long browns for lunch. We built a fire to fry the fish and ate them with bread spread with margarine. My wife's fish slipped off her plate and fell into the dust beside the fire. No matter. I picked up my rod which I had left resting against a tree and walked twenty feet to the river. A minute later I caught another trout—a rainbow—cleaned it, and put it into the pan. It was that kind of a day.

After lunch we sat and read beneath the cottonwoods and played with Adam on the little beach that had formed where a sandy arroyo entered the stream. We took a walk along the stream in the late afternoon. On the way back to the campsite we gathered firewood. The shadows were lengthening as we made a fire. Trout began to rise again.

After dinner we sat around the fire and ate chocolate chip cookies, watching nightfall. Adam was very tired. I tucked him into his sleeping bag in the tent. He lay with his head on Woof, a stuffed dog he had gotten for his first birthday. He asked me questions about numbers. I sang to him. He went to sleep. I listened to him breathe, slow and steady. Then I went back to the fire.

Randy and I sat and watched the flames and talked about the hummingbirds. The fire died. Coals glowed. There was no moon. The sky was dark and filled with stars. We listened to the river. Trout were still rising. I could hear the soft splashes above the sound of the river. It grew cold. Randy went to the tent and readied herself for sleep. I went down to the river and got some water to drown the coals. Then I followed her to bed.

The next morning I rose early again. The day was a carbon copy of the one before. The sky was cloudless and blue. The air was cold, and I waited expectantly as the sun climbed above the bare hills and its light moved down the pine-covered hillside to the river. But when the sunlight reached the river there were no clouds of insects, and there were no hummingbirds. As the day warmed a few of the big gray mayflies floated down the surface of the river, but only a few. Occasionally a trout would rise to take one of the large insects, but rising trout were few and far between. I fished again, and I caught some trout, enough for lunch and dinner when we returned home. It was a good day by most standards, but measured against the day before, the Los Pinos seemed almost lifeless.

On Monday when I returned to the office, I could not get the river and Saturday morning out of my mind. Sitting at my desk, glistening clouds of insects rose and fell above the surface. Big mayflies floated in the current. Trout rose to take them. The sun was golden on the bare hills. The smell of the cottonwoods was sweet and strong. That evening after Adam had gone to sleep I wrote a letter to a fishing buddy in Pennsylvania describing the hummingbirds, the richness of the river, the hatches and the multitudes of rising trout. Writing that letter, I relived the day again as I have done many times since that July morning. Days like that do not come often.

Several times in the years that followed, I had the good fortune to fish the Los Pinos again. The river was always beautiful, and every time I fished it I caught trout. As the years passed I came to value the wild browns more and the stocked rainbows less. I camped with my sons by the river. Sometimes the sun shone and sometimes it rained. Once Adam and I were tormented by mosquitoes, a rare occurrence in New Mexico, and drove twenty miles to Antonito for insect repellant and ice cream sundaes. I had good days and I had a few when the fishing was pretty slow. But even the best days did not compare with the day of the hummingbirds. Which is probably as it should be.

There are days when the richness of nature and your own good fortune assault your senses. Days when game fills the woods and birds fill the air. Days when the meadows are bright with wildflowers and butterflies. Days when insects hatch in clouds and the trout throw caution to the winds. But those days are few and far between. In nearly three decades of fly fishing, I have had only a handful. I remember them all.

On a summer night beside a big lake in British Columbia, we woke to the awful feeling of insects crawling on our bodies. They were carpenter ants, black and nearly an inch long. In the morning we could see them along the logs and dead wood by the lake. Many fell in the water. Trout cruised the shallows sipping the insects. I tied some crude imitations using black wool to form a small ball in the front of the hook and a larger one near the rear to mimic the shape of the ants' bodies. Standing on the shore, we could pick a trout from among the dozens that swam along the shoreline, cast the fly ahead of the fish, and watch as the trout inhaled the fly. We caught nearly a hundred trout, which we salted and smoked in a makeshift smokehouse we fashioned that night out of two old steel drums and a length of stovepipe.

Several years later, on a Memorial Day weekend, my friend Jon and I fished Kettle Creek in north-central Pennsylvania. We had both worked late and did not reach the stream until the wee hours of Saturday morning. When we got there we were too tired to pitch a tent, so we pulled off the road and rolled out our sleeping bags beside the river. In the morning, we woke and immediately began to fish. While Jon was putting on his waders, I started casting. By the time he came down to the river, I had taken two seventeen-inch browns. Jon walked to the head of the pool I was fishing and immediately proceeded to take a dozen trout on as many casts. One hatch after another blanketed the creek for the next three days, including big green drakes. On the first day, I caught dozens of trout. On the second day, I started focusing on big fish and caught my first twenty-inch trout on a fly. By the time Monday evening rolled around, I had caught three of them.

There are people who chase days like the day of the hummingbirds across the globe. That pursuit is not for me, even if I could afford it, which I can't. I would be lying if I told you that I did not long for more days like that. The hope is in the back of my mind every time I fish. But secretly, sometimes even from myself, I am glad that they do not come too often. I like the searching for and stalking of shy fish, the mix of observation, caution, and skill that an ordinary day on an ordinary stream demands. It is not a puritannical belief that there is virtue in working hard for small rewards or that there is something wrong with having great success with little effort. It is not the sense of accomplishment that comes from taking fish under difficult conditions. It is not even the intuition that an endless series of fifty-fish days would be a kind of purgatory, ultimately numbing rather than gratifying. Rather, I think, it is that I like the hunting game too well.

We are by nature problem solvers and wonderers, and the hunt is a very old puzzle. There is something in me that comes alive when I must look very hard and deep to find the fish in the river and move silently so they do not flee and cast so that my fly lights on the water as gently as an insect borne by the wind. It is something very old and deep. It is something that I cannot easily name. I did not learn it at school or in a book. It is something that I do not use in my urban life. It is a heightening of the senses, a sharpening of sight, smell, and sound. It is a deepening wonder at the complexity of the natural world. It is a profound respect for the creatures with whom we share the earth. And it is strongest on ordinary days on ordinary rivers.

When I take to the stream, it is always with the knowledge and the hope that anything is possible, that the day may bring hatches so thick that they draw the hummingbirds from the trees. Usually, it does not end up that way. Usually, I have to search the margins of the stream for the odd rising trout. Usually, there is no hatch and I can only guess at what unseen insect has drawn it to the surface. Then a day comes along. It begins like any other day. But something is different. The river is alive. Fish are everywhere. All the knowledge gained on all the ordinary days on ordinary rivers is unconscious, but it is part of you. You see the trout and hear them and know how to take them. It does not happen often, but it does happen. And when it happens you remember it forever.

*Chapter Four*

# EL PORVENIR CANYON

"Most scenic canyon in state; good fishing, numerous beaver dams. Accessible by trail only." That was how the *Guide to New Mexico Fishing Waters* described El Porvenir Canyon. I had been there once in winter. A foot of wet snow lay on the ground. I walked a half-mile up the canyon before turning back. It was enough to convince me that at least as far as the scenery was concerned, whoever wrote the guide meant what he said. The creek was iced over and I didn't see any beaver dams. It was hard to tell about the fishing. I told myself that I would return in the spring to find out.

A few years later I did. Danny went with me. He had just turned four. It was a windy spring morning. As we drove east along the interstate around the southern end of the Sangre de Cristos, wind rippled the brown grass and shook the chamisa. Small white clouds drifted across the mountains. The trip to El Porvenir Canyon was longer than I remembered. By the time we turned off the highway at Las Vegas, Danny had listened to both sides of his Sesame Street tape. He was cranky and sleepy. I needed to do something to cheer him up, so I told him that I would carry him in the backpack when we got to the trail. That helped, but only a little.

There were a half-dozen pickup trucks parked at the trailhead when we finally got there. Danny's mood changed as soon as he got out of the car and saw the rushing stream and the little bridge that crossed it next to the parking area. He played on the bridge and threw sticks and pebbles into the water while I put extra clothes for him and lunch into the backpack. Before putting a box of flies into the pack, I selected a size fourteen hair wing caddis with a green body that I had tied a few nights earlier and knotted it onto the leader on my small fly rod. Danny was jumping off a rock doing karate kicks in the air when I called and told him we were going to start walking up the creek. I asked him if he wanted to walk. He didn't. Instead he said he wanted to ride in the backpack. I put him in the pack and headed up the trail.

Danny was heavier than I remembered. He was growing fast. This would be the last summer I would carry him. The thought made me sad. From the time he was a few months old I had carried him on walks through the woods. We had begun with Sunday morning hikes along the Bear Wallow Trail, when we left the sleeping house and drove to the trail head on the Ski Basin road. I would hike the four-mile circuit with Danny in a pack against my stomach, alternately smiling at the forest and dozing.

By fall we were taking longer hikes and he was reaching for branches and leaves as we walked. When Danny was six months old I took him to Panchuela Creek in the Pecos where he ate his first solid food. It had been a beautiful October afternoon. The creek was low and clear. The sun was warm. Leaves floated in the water, brown trout rose to my flies, and we stayed so late that my wife called the State Police and reported us missing. When Danny could sit upright he began riding in a backpack. Our walks grew longer. Together we had worn out one backpack and were well on the way to wearing out a second.

Danny had grown into a bold and agile little boy. He was a good walker, but riding in the pack was still special. I wanted his feelings about walking along small streams in the woods to be special too. So I carried the heavy pack and listened to the music of his talk about ninja turtles and video game "endguys" and felt his hands on my shoulders and walked along the shaded path beside the rushing stream in the cool of a late April morning.

After a short while we came to a series of deep pools. I passed the first two, but when we reached the third I stopped and looked over the water from the high bank. The creek was high and tinged greenish brown. I could see five trout resting near the surface in the slow current. I pointed the fish out to Danny. He said he saw them, but I wondered if he really did. He did not have the benefit of polarized sunglasses. I did. Still, there was not much that Danny didn't see. Adam was always amazed at how observant his younger brother was. He said Danny had "eagle eyes."

The pool was long and slow and filled with dead timber. Near the far bank, behind a tree trunk that lay at right angles across the stream, a pale fish finned lazily in the current. It was larger than the other trout that were visible in the pool. I showed the fish to Danny and told him I was going to try to catch it. He became very still in the pack. I could feel him watching. Threading my backcast through the trees, I cast. Although the fish was no more than twenty feet away, the fly fell far short.

Before I could pick it up to cast again, a trout hit. The fish rocketed into the air three times and then came quickly to the bank. I lifted it out of the water. The trout was an eight-inch brown, dark and thin but healthy. Danny asked if we could keep it. I told him that we were going to release this fish so that it could grow and that we would release all the fish we caught unless we got a good one in the afternoon just before we left. I asked Danny if he wanted to touch the trout before I released it. He said he did, and he held it gently for a few seconds before giving it back to me. I released the trout and we watched it swim slowly into the deeper water and disappear.

The pale fish was still holding in the slack water below the drowned tree trunk. It took me a few casts to get the fly under an overhanging branch where it could drift slowly downstream to the trout, but on the first good cast the fish rose lazily and inhaled the fly. I set the hook and the fish came to me almost without a struggle. He was a foot-long male brown, all head and thin as a snake, still not recovered from spawning in the fall. I released him quickly. There were other fish still visible in the pool but I wanted to see more of the canyon before lunch so we headed upstream.

As we walked along the trail Danny chattered merrily about video games and Nintendo, imaginary battles and school friends. "Me and Ryan didn't do the rules last year," he told me. I could hear the laughter in his voice, but it took me a while to figure out what he meant. It turned out to be that he and his friend Ryan had decided that it was against the rules to "hide" under the piano bench in nursery school. They thought it was very mischievous and that they were getting away with something. Debbie, their teacher, thought it was harmless fun and let them get away with it every time. The words "last year" could mean yesterday or a month ago. Time was still a mystery.

The trail was gentle and wide. Twice it crossed the stream at shallow fords where I could step from stone to stone across the rushing water. The rocks were slippery, and I had to move carefully to keep my balance. At the third crossing there was no shallow chain of rocks across the creek, and I went in over the tops of my boots. Icy water soaked my feet.

The stream was high with melting snow from the high country, but the trail was bone dry. Even in the shadiest spots no snow lay on the ground. It did not augur well for summer. In my five years in New Mexico, even after dry winters the trails had always been muddy in the spring. Not this year. Without a rainy spring and summer, all of us, trout and bears, trees and men, would be in trouble. It was a slender thread that sustained us.

Pink granite cliffs rose above the path, visible through the tall ponderosa pines that grew in the canyon. I could see pine trees on the tops of the cliffs three thousand feet above us. I wondered how they survived. Some of the ponderosa pines along the stream were enormous. They towered a hundred feet or more above our heads. I pointed out a real giant to Danny. He looked up at it for a long time and then announced that he was hungry and wanted to eat lunch. I said I wanted to find a sunny spot next to the stream. He agreed. He said he wanted the sunny spot next to the stream to have big rocks to sit on. I agreed. A moment later we found it. And just above our sunny spot next to the stream with big rocks to sit on was a deep pool.

After I had taken Danny out of the pack, we sat by the stream and ate crackers, cheese, bagels, and cookies and drank water from the canteen. High in the trees the wind was blowing harder, but the tall pines sheltered us from its force. The sound of the wind mingled with the rush of the stream. Clouds rolled over the thin slice of sky between the treetops and the granite cliffs. When the clouds obscured the sun it would grow suddenly cold and foreboding. Then the clouds would blow away and our rock would be drenched in sunlight. Danny sat on my lap. We chewed our cookies without speaking.

When he had finished eating, Danny got up and began sorting through a tangle of sticks that the previous year's high water had lodged between two boulders. After a moment he found what he was looking for, a foot-long stick with a handle like a gun. He climbed a boulder and began firing at imaginary targets. I watched him play. What did he see, I wondered. I tried to remember myself at his age. It was too far away. The big rock in the park that had been my "fort" when I was a child was still clear in my mind, but I couldn't remember what I had played or the feelings that had gone with the game. Danny's gun had been replaced by a longer stick, a sword. He was fighting a duel with a small bush that grew on the bank. He was laughing. I rose and got my rod.

After making my way to a big flat rock in the middle of the stream, I looked out over the pool. It was perfect. The stream sluiced into the head of the pool and carved a deep hole along the edge of a great dark boulder before spreading out and gliding up against a natural dam of rocks. The water was deep and slow. It looked like it should have held some big fish, but all I could see were a lot of small ones. Trout finned lazily a few inches beneath the surface. Sometimes one would move purposefully to the side to ingest some bit of food drifting beneath the surface. Then it would return to its place in the stream.

I shook loose some line so that I could make a cast and the little green caddis fly fell on the surface just above the dam. Before I could lift the fly to cast a trout rose and hit the fly hard, hooking himself. It was another small brown, dark and thin like the others.

After releasing the trout I turned and looked for Danny. He was nowhere to be seen. A moment of panic. I called his name. Before he could answer, I saw the stick, protruding from behind a boulder and moving toward me. Then Danny appeared. I asked him if he wanted to reel in a trout, and he said he did. Two more casts and another trout struck. Although the fish looked like a good one, Danny reeled it in without much of a struggle. It turned out to be a spawned out male with a big head and not much else. Danny held the fish for a moment before we released him. The trout struggled in the current and then slowly swam away. I felt slightly guilty for adding to his troubles. I hoped he would make it.

Danny and I climbed back up the bank to the trail. For twenty minutes we walked up along the stream holding hands. In his free hand Danny held his "gun." He fired at enemies in the woods. I listened to the stream and the wind in the trees. More and more clouds passed overhead, and finally the sun was gone. The woods were cold and dark. It was time for us to turn around and start back to the car. It was a long way back to the car, too long for Danny to walk the whole way and too long for me to carry him. So I decided to try playing a game while we walked to take Danny's mind off how tired he was.

On the way back we counted. First we counted to a hundred, alternating numbers. Danny said, "One." I said, "Two." He said, "Three." And so it went, with a few hitches, up to a hundred. After the third time we counted to a hundred Danny said, "Now let's mess up. You first. One." "Two." "Three." "Seven!" When I said seven, Danny laughed until I thought his sides were going to split. Then he announced, "Now it's my turn. One." "Two." "Three." "Four." "A zillion three hundred and twenty-thirteen!" he said, laughing so hard the words could hardly escape his mouth.

Next it was my turn. "One-two," I said. "Two-three," he replied. "Three-four." "Four-five." We didn't quite get to a hundred, but we did get a long way back down the trail before Danny tired of the game and asked me to put him in the pack.

As we followed the trail back down toward the car the canyon floor grew wider. Dead fallen trees were all around us. The stream flowed placidly over a light bottom of sand and silt. I looked at the fallen trees. They had been cut down by beavers a long time ago. The bare wood that had been exposed by the beavers' teeth was silver with age. Hundreds of trees had been felled ranging from saplings to trees nearly two feet in diameter.

And then I saw it. A low ridge spanned the width of the canyon floor at right angles to the stream. At first I couldn't believe it, but my eyes didn't lie. Where the stream cut through the ridge, sticks and twigs and branches were laid bare. The ridge, more than fifty yards of it, was what remained of an enormous beaver dam. The beavers were long gone, and earth and pine needles covered their handiwork, but the dam was unmistakable. I wondered how I could have missed it on our way upstream. Perhaps I had been watching the stream too closely, looking for trout, to see anything but the water. Perhaps the dam was less apparent from below. You often see things differently when you look at them from another angle. It never ceases to amaze me how many new pockets and holding lies I see when I fish down the same stretch that I have just fished up or when I fish the same water from the opposite bank.

I pointed out the dam to Danny and explained how the beavers had built the dam using sticks they had cut with their teeth. I told him that the dam had blocked the flow of the creek and created a shallow lake that had once stretched back up the flat canyon floor. He asked to see a beaver. They were gone, and all I could show him were the marks of their teeth on the stumps of dead trees. He asked me why the beavers had built the dam. I told him it was for protection against their enemies. Beavers were good swimmers, and most of their enemies were not. In the shallow lake the beavers had been safe.

It was an eerie place. How long ago had the beavers lived there, I wondered, and why had they left? It was a question sometimes asked about men. The country to the west was filled with such places: Chaco Canyon, Mesa Verde, Canyon de Chelly—the ruined centers of a civilization that had once flourished in the dry country of the Southwest. The Anasazi had left them nearly a thousand years ago. No one knew why. Some attributed the desertion of the great centers to changes in the climate. Some said that the Anasazi had exhausted the resources on which their economy was based. Some argued that enemies had driven them away. But these were only theories. No one really knew.

The same reasons might explain why the beavers were gone and their dam stood in ruins. Perhaps a dry spell had led them to leave the dam or a flash flood had ruptured it beyond repair. Perhaps they had exhausted the food supply within reach of the dam and been forced to move on. Perhaps they had been killed by men or other predators. At the core of things the mystery of the dam was the same as that of Chaco and Canyon de Chelly. I did not know why the dam was deserted. I could only guess.

I thought about my house. I wondered what would be left of it in a thousand years. I drew a blank. It was too remote. A hundred years then. Would it still be there? It was a murky picture. I could see for a year, five years, maybe even ten and then time became an abstraction and change beyond my ability to imagine. In the short run, the odds were good that change would be incremental. I might put up some bookcases or build a new fence. There would be more houses and stores and businesses in the city. Neighborhoods would change. In some places commercial development would replace homes. There would be more demand for water and other resources. That much I knew.

But in the long run the changes would be more profound and more difficult to foresee. The land around the city was dry. The supply of water was finite. What would happen when demand exceeded supply? That time was probably not far off. Would parts of the city die? Would we deal with the problem before it reached crisis proportions? Probably not, if the past was any guide. The only certainty was that one day my house would be gone. I wondered if some traveler in the unseen future would pass by, see a small toy half-hidden in the earth, and wonder what lives had been lived where my home once stood.

I looked at the place where the stream cut through the ridge exposing the past and tried to picture the lake along the canyon floor, but all I could see was the ruined dam. I was glad when Danny announced that he was sleepy and wanted to go back to the car. It was time to go home.

By the time we reached the car my shoulders and legs ached. When I took off the pack, my back was soaked with sweat. Relieved of the burden, I felt almost weightless as I loaded the car and got ready to leave. After putting Danny in his car seat and stowing the rest of the gear in the trunk, I sat down in the car and breathed a long sigh. Then we drove back down to Las Vegas through Gallinas Canyon. It was lower and drier than where we had been. There was space between the ponderosa pines here and the dry ground showed the country was not far removed from desert. As we left the mountains, the clouds thinned and the skies cleared. When we reached Las Vegas the town was in brilliant sunlight.

Before we got to the highway Danny asked me if I would buy him a Dr. Pepper and some chocolate chip cookies at McDonald's. I did and picked up a cup of black coffee for myself. Then we headed out onto the highway. In a moment Danny was asleep. While he slept a storm raged in the mountains to the north. Lightning flashed and the peaks were hidden in black clouds. Danny's face was soft and very young. He was still sleeping when we reached home.

*Chapter Five*

# TRUJILLO MEADOW

On a sunny mid-September day I was driving along a dirt track in southern Colorado on my way to the headwaters of the Rio de los Pinos. The way I read the map, the road I was on ran parallel to the Los Pinos for several miles before finally descending to meet the unseen stream. It was a warm morning in the high country. The windows were open. The air was clean and sweet. The aspens were beginning to turn. After a long ride in a noisy old car, I was ready to do some fishing. The stream was supposed to be loaded with wild trout. I had a sleeping bag, tent, and lots of food in the car. Like the beer commercial says, "It doesn't get any better than this."

And then I realized I was on the wrong road. It was not a particularly brilliant realization. Instead of dropping down to meet the river, the road climbed and grew steadily rougher until it degenerated into a logged-out hillside of stumps and mud, imprinted with the tracks of heavy machinery. In my old Datsun it was impassable. No harm done. All I needed to do was turn around and figure out where I had gone wrong.

As I backed up the car to turn around I felt it hit something hard and heard the sound of metal scraping rock under the rear end. Suddenly I didn't feel so good anymore. I stopped the car and looked underneath. Oil was seeping slowly from the differential. It didn't look too bad, but it was clear that I wasn't going to spend the night in the mountains. Getting home would be the priority for the rest of the day. I turned the car around and drove slowly, very slowly, back to the dirt road that led to the highway.

Shortly after I turned onto the gravel forest road I came upon a sign that read, "Trujillo Meadow Reservoir 1 Mile." The name "Trujillo Meadow" rang a bell. At first I couldn't remember what it was, but then it came back to me. At some point during the previous winter, we had eaten dinner at Matt and Sue's house. After dinner, Matt and I gazed at a national forest map. It was the kind of thing you do in late winter, when you've been cooped up inside for too long and the snow is still heavy in the high country, but you can feel the days starting to lengthen. We talked and daydreamed about places on the map, places we had been and places we wanted to see when the snows melted. And Matt had pointed to Trujillo Meadow on the map. It was a small reservoir formed by a dam on upper Los Pinos. Trujillo Meadow had been the jumping off place for an elk hunt he had gone on years earlier. He talked about the hunt, the beauty of the country, and the many small streams filled with trout. I couldn't remember whether he got an elk. But I remembered what he had said about the fishing.

I stopped the car and crawled underneath. Maybe the leak wasn't so bad after all. I decided to drive to the reservoir and eat lunch there. After all, I had to eat lunch somewhere, right? The day would not be a total loss.

Five minutes later I drove down a pine covered hillside and saw the Los Pinos, a clear shallow stream running through a brushy meadow into a small lake. I slowed down to get a better look. A ring appeared at the tail of a flat pool. A moment later there was another and then a third. I stopped the car. Even from a distance of a hundred yards I could see that there were a lot of fish in that pool. I got out of the car and made my way through the tall grass and bushes toward the stream. Fifty feet from the bank I circled down below the pool where I had seen fish rising. After pausing for a moment, I began to move slowly up the bank, crouching low and watching the water. And then I saw the fish.

Brook trout! The pool was full of them. In the clear shallow water I could see the red of their flanks and the orange and white piping on their fins. They finned nervously in a run of deeper water by the far bank and in the sunlit tail of the pool. I took a step closer. The trout seemed to tense. I waited and then moved forward. The trout fled in alarm up the stream leaving wakes as they rushed upstream through a three-inch deep riffle into the next pool.

I turned and looked down toward the lake. As I did, another group of perhaps twenty trout splashed up through a shallow run into the pool beside which I stood. I did not move, and the trout did not see me. The new arrivals took much the same positions in the pool as their departed brethren. They were edgy and excited. They had good reason to be on edge. In the shallow open stream at midday the trout were exposed and vulnerable. I stood very still. The trout did not see me. Then I moved and the trout raced away.

Eventually I followed the stream down to where it flowed into the lake. Every pool held trout. According to what I had heard and read, the trout in the Los Pinos were supposed to be browns, but all the fish I saw were brook trout. And what brook trout. These were not the shy little fish that lived in the shaded springs and seeps along the streams I fished in New York and Pennsylvania years earlier. Instead they were fine, heavy fish, ranging from a foot to fourteen or fifteen inches in length.

As I walked toward the lake, fish were moving up the stream leaving wakes in the riffles. When I reached the little inlet where the Los Pinos flowed into the reservoir, dozens of fish swam in seemingly aimless circles. Every few minutes, a small group of fish would break from the milling school and enter the stream, racing through the shallow mud-bottomed flat into the brightly flowing water of the Los Pinos, an endless parade of trout moving from the lake to the river. I watched spellbound for a long time.

Suddenly I was hit by an attack of buck fever. There were hundreds of good-sized brook trout in the little stream that ran by my feet. There was a fly rod in my car. What was I waiting for? I turned and jogged back through the meadow to the car. As I moved through the long grass and brush, grasshoppers shot out from under my feet. A hopper pattern would be the first fly I would try.

When I got back to the car I remembered the leaky differential. Maybe it wasn't that bad after all. Oil was still seeping out, but the wet spot under the car was pretty small. I did a quick mental balancing act comparing a night stranded in the mountains against a stream filled with brook trout. It was no contest. The differential would have to wait.

I ate lunch sitting on the Datsun's fender. An apple, some cheese, and a few cookies followed by a long drink of water. The day was getting hot, and this was no time to get dehydrated. Then I took my small rod out of the trunk and rigged it as fast as I could. When it came time to tie on the fly, I noticed that my hands were shaking. In the small pools all along the Los Pinos, fish were still rippling the surface, and I could see their wakes in the shallows as they moved up the stream.

I trotted back down to the Los Pinos. When I neared the water I slowed. The dark forms of a dozen trout were visible against the pale bottom of a shallow pool. I approached carefully from below, crouching low and keeping well away from the water to conceal myself from the fish. A half dozen trout were holding tight to the near bank fifteen feet upstream. I let out line slowly, made two false casts and then dropped the hopper six inches from the bank and a few feet above the furthest fish. The fly drifted down with the current toward the fish. It was a perfect drift, slow and drag free. My muscles tensed. The fly floated over one fish, then another and then a third until it had passed them all. The fish didn't move. Another cast brought the same result. A third cast and still . . . nothing. It was as if the fly wasn't there. Finally, on the fourth cast I dumped the hopper and a pile of line with a splash in the middle of the trout. They took off in all directions, coalesced as a group and then raced upstream.

The same performance was repeated in a half-dozen other pools with an equal number of fly patterns, large and small, wet and dry, imitations and attractors. In each case the response was the same. The trout ignored my offerings until I made a bad cast. Then they panicked and fled. With each successive pool, the bad casts seemed to come sooner. It was frustrating fishing.

Things were a lot less frustrating for the fish. Here and there, in the graveled heads and tails of pools, fish were spawning. Males jostled for position beside females. Shuddering sides of trout expelling eggs and milt flashed in the afternoon sun. It was a microcosm of the great salmon runs of the Northwest. I should have had enough sense to get my camera from the car or just sit on the bank and watch the spectacle, but I didn't.

Instead, I kept on fishing, making my way slowly up the stream. Finally, I lucked out. The hopper disappeared in a splash and I was fast to a good trout. In the shallow stream the fish was no match for even the featherweight rod, and I quickly hoisted her onto the bank. She was a female brook trout, a foot long, sleek and heavy. I killed her with a blow from a rock, admired her and put her in my creel. Then I continued up the stream.

The afternoon sun grew hot. The sky was an intense deep blue. Two hawks circled on the still air, searching the meadow for prey. When their shadows crossed the stream, the trout raced for the shelter of undercut banks. There they hid for long moments before tentatively venturing out again into open water. The urge to live was stronger than the urge to reproduce. I thought about it and decided that the trout were taking the long view, that it was necessary to survive the moment for life to go on in the long run. And then I fished some more.

That afternoon I fished long and hard over more trout than I had ever seen. The fish ignored good casts and fled in terror from bad ones, only to return a moment later and resume their amorous play. Food seemed to be the last thing on their minds. The "rises" I could see were fish disturbing the surface of the stream as they jostled for mates or moved through the shallows. Not once did I see a trout take an insect from the surface.

Late in the day I came to a place where the stream made a bend and formed a pool. At the head of the pool, by the far bank, there was a small eddy of clear slack water. In the eddy were two pairs of trout. One of the fish, a male, was larger and broader than any fish I had seen. I wanted that trout badly. So I tried a hopper pattern. No interest. I tried an ant. No interest. A caddis nymph, a hare's ear, a small black streamer. Nothing worked. I tied on a brown wooly worm, cast it out and drifted it through the eddy. The trout did not move.

\* \* \*

I grew up in the 1950s, a time when fishing was not an abstract sport. When I fished with my father, we fished for pleasure, but no trip was ever considered a success unless we caught fish and lots of them. Fish were food, and releasing a legal fish was akin to throwing away food. It was something that we just didn't do. I cannot recall my father ever releasing a fish that was of legal length. No matter how many fish we caught—and the fishing regulations in those years allowed us to keep huge numbers of fish—we kept them all. And no fish that we kept ever went to waste. We ate what we caught. If we caught more than we could eat, we invited company for dinner or cleaned the fish and gave them to non-fishing friends who were always happy to have them.

Cleaning fish was an integral part of every fishing trip. Like most people, my father did not look on cleaning a mess of fish as one of life's pleasures. But my father was nobody's fool. He had a son who loved everything about fish and fishing. Everything. And so when I was very young, he taught me how to clean fish and led me to believe that it was a fine and honorable activity and the culmination of every successful fishing trip. On some level I believe it still.

The moral code of my childhood was that a fish not killed and cleaned was a fish wasted. That is powerful stuff, and it stays with you long after the world has changed and you know that the old rules no longer make sense. I suspect that it goes even deeper than that. We were hunters even before we were fully human, and we became human, at least in part, through the hunt. Fishing is not just about a nice day in the outdoors. It is not just about maintaining contact with the natural world. It is about a very specific kind of contact. It is about the hunt. It is about predation. It is about catching fish.

\* \* \*

I wanted the big trout very badly, and the trout was not interested in any of the flies I had to offer. Artful presentation and finely tied flies would not take this fish. The trout was too preoccupied with spawning and too nervous in the shallow open water to care about food. And then something took over. I knew what I was going to do was wrong, but I did it anyway. I cast the heavily weighted fly into the eddy two feet above the trout. It sank to the bottom slightly upstream of the fish. The leader draped over his back. I let out a long slow breath. The fish did not move. Then I gave a sharp tug on the line, driving the fly into the trout. When the hook penetrated his side, the trout zigzagged back and forth, circled the pool a few times and then gave up. I lifted him onto the high bank and felt a surge of triumph. It was short-lived.

The fish lay on the grass breathing heavily. He was long and deep, and he was very beautiful. Black back with white vermiculations shading into deep green spotted with red and blue and yellow. Then red-orange sides, a thin black line, and pure white belly. His orange fins were edged with white and black. The fly was lodged in his side. A trickle of blood oozed from the wound. He gasped for breath. The sight of him lying there took all the joy out of me. I desperately wanted the trout to live. I felt guilty and ashamed and confused.

* * *

A father's shadow is always long. It is especially long when your father is wise and strong and loving. And it is longer still when he dies, as my father did, just before you have gone through the rebellious years of adolescence, cut the cord and made your truce, if not as equals then at least as separate adults. My father has always occupied a place slightly larger than life, a place somewhere between memory and myth. But watching the trout lying in the grass on the bank of the Los Pinos I took a step out of the shadow.

My father grew up in one world and I now lived in another. He grew up in the old world. I lived in the new. He came of age in a time long before the writings of Aldo Leopold and Rachel Carson and others documented the devastating impact of civilization on the natural world. I read them all. He fished in rivers of comparative plenty. In my life, such rivers were few and far between. He was born at the turn of the twentieth century, at a time when the earth's resources appeared, if not limitless, then at least abundant. I was living in a time when the planet sometimes seemed to shrink before my eyes, when resources as basic as water were increasingly in short supply and when life forms were disappearing at a rate that rivaled the great extinctions of the geological past. His was a world of full stringers. Mine was a world of catch and release. His views were shaped by his time. My views were shaped by mine.

But my father's vision of fishing encompassed more than catching and keeping lots of fish. He abhorred waste. I can never recall him fishing for spawning fish. He thought ill of catching bass on their beds in the spring. And he lived in an era of short open seasons, which he observed, when freshwater fishing began in April and ended in September. Likewise, he released fish that were below the legal size, and he never kept more than his limit. Still, he fished to catch fish. He usually used bait in preference to lures because he thought it more effective, and I can recall him "sweetening" wet flies with thin strips of bacon rind on a day when the brook trout in a Quebec pond restricted to fly fishing were singularly uncooperative. But in general, he played by the rules and scrupulously observed those that were thought to preserve fish stocks according to the prevailing wisdom of the day.

So playing by the rules was part of the game too, and over the years since my father's death the rules, both society's and my own internal ones, had become more complex. I moved from warm water fish to trout. I learned how to drift worms down through the holding water of Catskill rivers without drag, first with a spinning rod and then with the fly rod my father bought me a year before he died. Then I began experimenting with dry flies in the pools and runs of Willowemoc Creek. Over time, flies replaced bait. Limits shrank. In places catch and release became the law of the river. My skills sharpened. I saw more. I became a hunter of fish in a way that my father had never been. I kept fewer fish, but I never stopped measuring success in terms of fish caught.

I do not mean to suggest that all these thoughts went through my mind in the brief seconds that the big brookie lay in the grass on the bank of the Los Pinos. It did not happen that way. But they were there nonetheless, somewhere below the threshold of consciousness, at the core of my conflict and confusion. My predatory instinct, part learned and part innate. My respect for the rules that restrained it. My love of the fish themselves. It was all there. All the years I had fished with my father. All the years of chasing trout alone, watching them in their streams and learning their ways. All the years of seeing homes and trailer parks and campgrounds go up on the banks of rivers I loved. And then it came together. I do not know what my father would have thought about snagging a single brook trout in a stream where there were thousands or what he would have done in that moment, but I knew what I thought, and I knew what I had to do, and that was what mattered.

* * *

A quick hard pull freed the hook from the trout's side. I lowered the fish gently back into the stream. He seemed disoriented at first. I held him in the current. I felt him gaining strength. With a flick of his tail he left my hand and swam steadily up across the pool back to the eddy and his mate. In a moment all was as before. Two pairs of trout were in the eddy. Others hung tight to the undercut bank. A new wave of fish splashed through the riffle at the tail of the pool. For several minutes I watched the wounded trout. He seemed okay. I hoped he was. Then I turned and slowly followed the little stream back down to the lake.

When I reached the lake there were two men there just getting ready to start fishing. "You see any fish in that little stream?" one of them asked. "No," I lied, "I don't think there are any in there. You'd be better off fishing the lake." With that I walked to my damaged car, packed away my rod and drove slowly back to Santa Fe. The car was less seriously wounded than I thought. It made it home and lived for another three years before finally succumbing to a cracked block. I hope that the trout did as well.

# Chapter Six

# THE FISHERMAN'S EYE

Last summer I went fishing with a friend on a small stream in the Jemez Mountains. I picked the stream with care. My friend had just taken up fly fishing, and I wanted to give him a chance to fish a stream with lots of unsophisticated trout. The stream I chose was secluded and seldom fished. It was loaded with wild cutthroats. They rose freely to dry flies, and they were not selective. I thought that it would be a morale booster. I was wrong.

After leaving the paved road we drove a dozen miles into the mountains. We parked the car in a grove of tall ponderosa pines at the rim of a canyon. It was shortly after noon. The sun was high in the sky, and far below we could see a thin ribbon of stream, glinting in the sunlight as it ran through a narrow opening in the forest that shaded the canyon floor.

The walk down to the stream took twenty minutes. At the trailhead there were only ponderosa pines, but as we descended into the canyon the foliage grew more diverse. There were stands of oak and aspen, and near the bottom Douglas firs rose high above the canyon floor. Cottonwoods and willows grew along the stream. Shafts of sunlight filtered down through the branches. The sound of moving water rose up to greet us. And then we were there.

The little creek was no more than six to eight feet wide in most places. It burbled along the canyon floor beneath a canopy of trees in a series of small pockets, pools, and runs. There was a pool where the trail met the stream. Near the head of the pool, I could see three small trout finning in the current. "Look," I said, "do you see those fish at the head of the pool?" "No. Where are they?" I pointed to the fish. He still didn't see them. "Watch," I said. I shook out a few feet of line and cast. A trout flashed at the elk hair caddis and missed. "Did you see that?" I asked. "No, what was it?" he answered. "Watch the fly," I said. I cast again. The bushy dry fly landed on the surface, drifted a foot and disappeared in a splash.

Seconds later, a small Rio Grande cutthroat was in my hand. The trout was perfectly formed, with a dark back, sides washed with pink and orange, rose gill covers and belly and black spots clustered toward its tail. My friend said it was the most beautiful fish he had ever seen. After we had admired the trout for a few seconds, I released it. For a moment the fish held in the shallows. Then it darted into the dark water beside a boulder and was gone.

We walked upstream together to the next pool. This time it was my friend's turn. He approached the pool slowly from below as I had told him to do. I could see a trout resting in the shallows at the tail of the pool. Six feet from the trout my friend stood straight to cast. The trout in the shallows darted up the pool leaving a vee-shaped wake. After a half dozen false casts the fly hit the water and drifted unmolested the length of the pool. My friend cast again. Nothing happened. Eventually he asked, "What did I do wrong?" "There was a trout in the tail of the pool. When you stood up to cast, you spooked it. Did you see it?" I replied.

My friend hadn't seen the trout he startled, and, try as he might, during the course of the afternoon, he failed to see many others. By the time the shadows started to grow long we had fished more than a mile of stream. I had caught and released nearly two dozen cutthroats. My friend had not had a single take. Casting in the close environs of a forested brook was second nature to me, but an endless succession of flies snagged in overhanging branches for my friend. And the fish that were in plain sight to me eluded my friend's vision. As we hiked back to the car, he told me that had I not pointed out dozens of trout to him, he would never have known they were there.

In his essay "The Deer Swath," Aldo Leopold wrote:

> . . . there are four categories of outdoors men: deer hunters, duck hunters, bird hunters, and non-hunters. These categories have nothing to do with sex or age, or accoutrements; they represent four diverse habits of the human eye. The deer

hunter habitually watches the next bend; the duck hunter habitually watches the skyline; the bird hunter watches the dog; the non-hunter does not watch. (223–24)

The same principle applies to fishing. The natural world is very rich and complex. There is more to see than we can absorb. Consciously or unconsciously we focus on certain things and filter out others. What we see is determined by our training, experience, and interests. A hiker walking along a stream might see only flowing water. An entomologist might see caddis flies dancing above the surface. A watchful fisherman might see a trout holding nearly motionless in a still pocket of water along the bank.

Seeing is much more than a matter of sharp eyesight, although it certainly helps. It is a complex of many things, including practice, desire, temperament, and knowledge. Some people also seem to be born with an innate knack for seeing in much the same way as some people are born with the innate ability to run fast, jump high, understand mathematics, or play the violin. The rest of us can improve our skills through devotion and hard work, but no amount of practice will ever enable us to play basketball like Michael Jordan or play the violin like Itzhak Perlman.

There is a boy I know, the son of friends, who seems to have been born with a special gift for seeing things. On a walk in the woods he always finds an antler, old horseshoe, or something more exotic that no one else has noticed. Once I took him and my son Danny for a walk along Holy Ghost Creek. The boys were still small. Danny was four. His friend was a year older. They played along the water's edge as I worked up the creek casting a dry fly into likely looking pockets and catching the occasional trout.

After eating lunch beside the stream, we headed back to the car. It was late June, the sun was warm, and the trail ran through meadows filled with wildflowers and buzzing insects. Suddenly the boy stopped and pointed at a patch of tall yellow flowers. "Look at that!" he said. I looked but saw only a patch of flowers no different than many others we had passed on our way. "Don't you see it?" he asked. "No," I said. "What is it?" The boy walked closer to the flowers. Danny and I followed. Then he pointed with his small hand to one of the flowers.

Something intricately colored and iridescent lay on the yellow petals. He picked it up. "Look," he said. It was a butterfly's wing.

Most of us, though, are not born with eyes like that. We have to learn to see. What we learn and how well we learn it depends mostly on a combination of practice and passion. If you spend time on rivers searching the water for trout, you will see their dark shadows against the lighter rocks and gravel of the river bottom. And if you fish long and hard, you will learn where in the river the trout are likely to lie, and you will look for them there. In time you will come to know something of how the trout live, what draws them, and what they fear. And if you really love the game, you will in time come to feel a part of yourself that you had forgotten, and you will move with caution and take the time to look more deeply into the waters. And you will see more.

Passion is important. It is the reason you are on the river. It is the reason you train your eyes on the river rather than the trees or the canyon wall. It is the reason you look down beneath its surface. It is the reason you search for the trout. But it is not enough. Knowledge shapes our vision. We need to know where to look in order to see.

Trout are not evenly distributed throughout a stream. Like other creatures they have needs and preferences that dictate where they are likely to be at any given time. These include shelter, food, protection from predators, and comfortable water temperatures. Streams are always flowing downhill. In order to maintain position in the river and avoid being swept downstream, trout must face up into the current and forever swim against it. Swimming against the current requires the trout to expend energy. If it expends more energy than it takes in, it will die. However, the current also brings with it a flow of insects on which the trout feed. These facts are important for two reasons. The first is that they dictate that trout will face upstream. The second is that in order to minimize their energy output and maximize their energy input, trout will seek out places in the river where they are sheltered from the full force of the current but still have ready access to the insects and other organisms the current brings.

To survive, trout also need protection from predators. Danger usually comes from above—ospreys, raccoons, and other creatures that patrol the river's edge looking for a meal. Safety for the trout might take the form of an undercut bank, a tangle of roots, or a deep broken-surfaced run. There are almost always trout in such places, but to see them you will have to look long and hard. Most of the time they are nearly invisible. They blend with the bottom of the stream. But if you watch carefully and you are lucky, a shadow on the bottom or the motion of a tail or fin may give the fish away, and then the trout will come into sharp relief, and you will wonder why you did not see it before.

Knowledge focuses our vision on the places in the river that meet the trout's needs because they are the places where trout are most likely to be. It also tells us how to approach them. Trout face upstream and food drifts down with the flow of the river. Danger comes from above. The trout's vision is directed upstream and upward. If you approach a trout from below and keep your silhouette low, the trout will not see you. Wild trout are survivors. They instinctively flee from sudden movements, loud noises, and strange shadows on the water. So when you approach you must move cautiously and quietly and avoid casting shadows on the water. But if you do it right, you can get very close to the fish.

Learning to see, however, is not just a matter of eyesight and training. Other senses come into play. When I am really fishing well I can hear things I do not normally hear. A splash behind me signals a rise. If I turn at the sound, I may see ripples spreading or catch a fleeting glance of the trout as it descends. But usually it is more subtle, a blip against the sound of the current, a momentary change in the cadence of the stream. Something makes me look for the source of the sound, and as often as not, it is a trout.

We humans observe the world mostly through sight and, to a lesser degree, through sound. Our sense of smell is not well developed. Still, more than one elk hunter has told me that you can sometimes catch the rank scent of the big deer on the wind and follow it to its source. And more than one charter boat captain has told me that he could sometimes smell a school of feeding bluefish even when the fish were feeding deep and there were no blues or baitfish breaking the surface and no diving seabirds to give them away. I have fished in lakes where certain coves just smelled "fishy." Often they were.

No matter how well and carefully you watch, there is a great deal that you will not see. The world is far too rich a place for our senses to take in more than a fraction of what there is for us to observe. Experience and the goals we pursue sharpen our focus but they also narrow our field of view. On that day when my friend and I fished the little creek in the Jemez, I saw the swirls and eddies of the current, the pockets and sheltered places in the stream, the insects that hovered above the water's surface and the trout. My friend, with his hiker's eye, saw the long sweep of the creek's surface as it ran along the canyon floor. Neither of us, I suspect, saw more than a fraction of the birds that flitted between the trees or glided across the blue slice of sky above the pale rocky walls. Neither of us noticed the small creatures that surely must have scurried along the forest floor.

At first glance it might seem that there is a trade-off. The fisherman who looks down into the river cannot see the birds in the air. By focusing his eye on the object of his sport, the fisherman gives up his ability to see other things. But that is not the way it works. There is a paradox here. Think back on what Aldo Leopold said. Different kinds of hunters watch different parts of the world around them. No matter how deeply and well they watch, each misses much of what the other sees. But, the more each kind of hunter focuses on his game and the part of the world it occupies, the more he sees. At the same time that it narrows his field of view, a passion for deer or ducks or trout sharpens the hunter's focus and increases the sum total of what he sees and knows.

It is not just that the fisherman sees the trout in the river while the casual observer does not. The fisherman sees more. He sees the rocks in the streambed, the flow and swirl of the current, the speed, depth, and clarity of the river. He sees the plants that wave in the water. He sees the interplay of light and shadow, the insects that move across the surface and through the vegetation on the bank. He sees the trees that line the banks. He feels the wind and watches its direction. He notices the place of the sun in the sky and the angle of his shadow. By focusing closely on one thing—the fish—he sees more, both of that thing and the whole interconnected natural world in which it lives and on which it depends.

"[T]he non-hunter does not watch." Thus, he does not see. Big Tesuque Creek is only a few miles outside of Santa Fe. The creek is filled with wild brown trout. The water is very clear except during runoff, and to a careful watcher, the trout are plainly visible as they rest in deep spots in the creek, along undercut banks and wherever they can find shelter from the current. On a summer day, a steady stream of hikers will walk along the creek. They may hear the noise of the creek as it spills over the rocks on its way down the mountain. They may see the dense vegetation along its banks. They may feel the coolness of its water. But not one in a hundred will ever notice the trout. To see them you must watch.

In introductory philosophy courses, instructors often ask whether a tree makes a noise when it falls in a forest if no one is there to hear. The one question is really two. The first is whether we can fairly assume from past observations of large objects falling that the falling tree makes a noise. The second is how we can prove that a particular tree made a noise when it fell if we did not observe the event. When I was eighteen, my answer to both questions was, "Who cares?" It was a flip kind of answer, a way of saying, "Don't bother me with this abstract nonsense. It has nothing to do with my life," but on at least one level it was the right answer. If you do not care, you will not see, and if you do not see, you will not know how things work. The order and the beauty of the world will escape you.

Most of what goes on in the natural world passes unnoticed except to those who care. Whatever significance it may have in some grand design escapes those who do not care. In order to observe wild things, you must care about them. If you do not care, you will not watch. The kind of watching that the fisherman does is not abstract. He is seeking a tangible connection with the fish, a connection with its life through the gossamer thread of the line that binds them to each other. The bond between fisherman and fish is a bond between predator and prey. It is a very old and deep bond. It is a bond that encourages and rewards watchfulness in a way you can touch and feel. It is a bond that draws upon powers of observation that find little use in a world increasingly based on money, computers, technology, and abstractions.

When the last hunter or fisherman passes from the scene, a large segment of the natural world will pass from human sight. There will be no one left with the desire to see it and no one left with eyes that can see.

*Chapter Seven*

# Rio Medio

My experiences on the Rio Medio are so conflicting and contradictory that I sometimes feel there are really two rivers at the bottom of the canyon below Borrego Mesa. One is a river that runs beneath tall trees past fields of flowers where jeweled trout rise to my fly from crystalline runs. The other is a stream littered with fallen trees, brushy and unfishable. When I make the drive to the trailhead at Borrego Mesa, I never know which river I will find.

The Rio Medio is a small river that drains the west slope of the Sangre de Cristo mountains just north of the village of Cundiyo. It is seldom more than fifteen feet wide, and outside New Mexico, a stream of similar size would be called a brook or perhaps a creek. To reach it, you take the paved road past Cundiyo, cross a bridge where the Rio Medio joins the Rio Frijoles, and then turn off onto a gravel forest road that winds up into the Sangre de Cristos toward Borrego Mesa campground. As the road rises, piñon and juniper give way to ponderosa pines, the pines grow taller and flowers appear by the roadside. The road crosses a great open meadow on a hilltop where horses graze and then re-enters the forest. Aspens mix with the pines. Moments later, a sign announces the turnoff for Borrego Mesa Campground.

Borrego Mesa Campground is a quiet place where grass and flowers grow on the open forest floor beneath tall stately pines. It is a small campground with horse corrals, and it is usually empty even in the height of summer. Two trails lead down to the Rio Medio from the mesa. The new trail descends the six hundred feet to the stream in a series of switchbacks. It is a good trail, well marked and well maintained. The old trail is very steep. It is badly eroded and you have to watch your step as you descend.

Halfway down, looking to the east, there is a view of an immense rounded peak in the heart of the Pecos wilderness. It is a place where I always feel very small, where I feel a tremor of fear and a kind of peace. The mountains surround me. They are steep-sided and dark. No trail or clearing or sign of human presence is visible, only end-less wooded mountains. When I stand there and look into the moun-tains, I am sometimes reminded of photographs my father took years ago, pictures of great vistas, cloud-filled skies, and lonely mountains, always with a small human figure silhouetted against the sky. There is an ancient resonance here, a memory of a time when we were small and few and the mountains and forests went on forever. In the canyon below an unseen river runs. On a quiet day, if the water is high, I can just make out the sound of the river. Then I descend. Minutes later, I am there.

The Rio Medio is small and perfect. Its canyon is deeply wooded with huge ponderosa pines and Douglas firs. Cottonwoods grow along the bank. The little river runs in shade. Its water is clear and icy. Much of the bottom is pale pebbles or light-colored rock. For a stream in the Sangre de Cristos it has a gentle gradient. In many places fallen trees, overhanging branches, and streamside brush con-spire to make it difficult to approach the water and impossible to cast. In these places a trout might not see a fly or a baited hook in the course of a season.

The trout are browns and Rio Grande cutthroats. They are bril-liantly colored fish. The combination of glass-clear water, pale bottom, and deep shade gives their colors a special intensity. The cutthroats are cutbows, cutthroat-rainbow hybrids. Often they have red-orange gill covers and sides. Occasionally one is pale, almost golden. They are unlike other Rio Grande cutthroats I have caught, but there is no mistaking them for rainbows. The crimson slashes beneath their gill covers and the large black spots on their backs, usu-ally clustered toward their tails, are a dead giveaway.

\* \* \*

One day when Adam was ten I took him to the Rio Medio. He did not say anything, but I sensed he did not want to go. I took him anyway. On the drive through the sculpted high desert north of Nambe, he sat sullen and stonefaced. When we reached the campground, he told me. He did not want to go. We started down the trail. It was a hot afternoon. Flies buzzed around our heads. Sweat ran down our faces. Again and again he told me, "I'm tired. I don't want to hike. When can we go home?"

I thought that when we reached the river things would change. I was wrong. He avoided the cool water and sat down on a log beside the trail where the sun beat down. Then he began to cry. I asked him why he was so sad. He told me he didn't know. His sadness was deep and nothing I could do or say seemed to help. Eventually, we began the long slow walk back up to the Mesa. When we reached the car, tears were running down his face. He was sound asleep by the time we reached the paved road. The sadness was still etched on his face.

* * *

A year later Adam and I returned to the Rio Medio on our almost annual backpacking trip. It was the Fourth of July weekend. I carried a heavy pack. He carried a small one. The woods were tranquil and empty and the morning air was cool and filled with the scent of pines. On our way down we met another father and son on horseback riding up out of the canyon, and later another pair of riders and two day hikers passed us on the trail as we neared the stream. They were the only people we saw in two days in the canyon. We stopped when we reached the river and took long drinks from a canteen and shared a candy bar. Then we put on our packs and followed the trail up along the Rio Medio.

We passed the log where Adam had sat and cried a year earlier. It was a place I would never forget, but he did not seem to recognize it. We talked about baseball and basketball. We looked for a campsite and eventually found what we were looking for in a small meadow bordered by tall fir trees and the river.

After setting up the tent, Adam and I searched our packs for a ball. Both of us had forgotten to bring one. I had two extra pairs of socks, though, so I suggested that we use a balled up sock as a base-ball. Adam was skeptical. So was I. To our surprise, it worked pretty well. The sock didn't go too far when the batter missed the pitch and it didn't go too far when the batter hit it. One-on-one baseball can be awfully boring if you have to spend most of your time chasing the ball instead of pitching and hitting. The sock never went far. We spent most of the afternoon playing baseball in the meadow by our campsite with a balled-up sock and a stick. When I told my wife about it she sort of shrugged, as if to say that men are weird.

Late in the afternoon, we built a fire by the stream on a sandy rock bank. Dinner was macaroni and cheese cooked on a Sterno stove that I had taken camping for twenty-five years. It had been with me for more than half my life. After dinner we tried to skip stones in the little stream. Adam doubted that he could do it, but in five min-utes he had it down and was trying to see how many rocks he could skip in a row. On the riffled surface using round river pebbles it was not easy. Eventually he did nine in a row.

We sat on a fallen log beside the fire and watched the flames as darkness fell. The sound of the Rio Medio drowned out the crack-ling of the fire, a deep bed of coals glowing red. We sat beside each other in the dark woods watching the fire die and listening to the river. Suddenly it was cold, and Adam said that he wanted to go to sleep. I filled the pot with icy water from the stream and drowned the fire. It was dark beneath the trees. Stars filled the open sky above the meadow.

In the tent we talked. Adam told me that there was one thing that he was scared of. Snakes, especially poisonous ones. He asked me if there were a lot of them in New Mexico. Yes, I told him, there are quite a few, but not here. Mostly you find them in the desert. Could there be any near our house, he asked, because, after all, we live in the desert. Yes, I told him, there could be snakes near our house, but it's not very likely. There are too many people where we live. People don't like snakes and would probably kill any poisonous ones they found. I felt I ought to put in a plug for snakes, say something about their role in the environment, but I couldn't bring myself to say any-thing good about them. I shared his revulsion. I was still thinking about it when I realized he was asleep.

I lay in the tent beside my sleeping son. I loved him so intensely. Why was it sometimes so hard to connect? Why did we fight? Would he find peace as he grew older? Would he find friends and happiness? We were so different, we two, and we were one. Why wouldn't he read books I knew he would love? I didn't either at that age, I remembered. Instead, I had prided myself on reading things that other people hadn't read. No, not at that age, but when I was older. But he was precocious in so many things. I watched him sleep and listened to the river.

The next morning after breakfast we hiked up the stream. The meadows along the Rio Medio were filled with large yellow flowers. Insects hummed. Caddis flies danced above the water in the heads of runs. Trout rose. We watched them but did not fish. We crossed the river on the trunk of a fallen tree. I showed Adam the tracks of a deer. We shared a chocolate bar on a rock by a small waterfall. Then we turned and walked back to the campsite. Just before we reached it I stopped to fish a deep fast run of water. On the first cast a foot-long brown nailed the fly. I cleaned it while Adam lit the stove. Fifteen minutes after the trout struck the fly it was on our plates. Adam ate most of it. He said it was the best fish he had ever eaten in his life.

After lunch we played baseball again with the balled up sock before taking down the tent. When the game was over, Adam sat on the log by the river and read while I washed the frying pan. When I finished, I joined him on the log. We sat together. I jotted down notes and watched the water while he read. By the far bank, no more than a dozen feet away, a small brown trout held in the lee of a protruding root. Periodically the trout would slide into the current, take some hapless insect and then dart back beneath the shelter of the root. I pointed out the fish to Adam. He watched it for a moment, nodded and then returned to his book.

A cloud slid across the sun and the air grew cool. The cloud passed and sunlight filled the meadow. In the distance thunder rumbled. I nudged Adam. It was time to go. We put on our packs and began the walk back along the stream. We stopped twice on the climb up out of the canyon. Adam was sweating and tired. We drank from the canteen and rested in the shade. Near the end of the climb, Adam asked me how much longer until we reach the car. Twenty minutes, I told him, thinking it was half that. Five minutes later we reached the stand of short twisted oaks that marked the end of the trail. Adam jogged the last hundred yards to the car.

We shared a chocolate bar and the last of our water before starting the drive home. It felt good to sit. Adam was asleep by the time we reached the paved road. His face was soft and smiling.

* * *

## JUNE 13, 1993

My knee and back bothered me on the hike down to the river. I also had trouble adjusting to my new bifocals. The trail at my feet was fuzzy and indistinct. I felt clumsy and inept. The river was high and I could hear it from the top of the mesa all the way down. It just kept getting louder. There was still lots of snow in the mountains above the river. Spring had been cold, but the past few days had been hot and the weather forecast was for more of the same. The earth was wet and in places water trickled across the trail. The air was warm and the smell of cottonwoods rose up out of the canyon as I descended. When I reached the river it was high, almost too high to fish. The water was roaring and fast and, at first, I saw few places for the fish to rest. But here and there, along the margins of the stream and behind big rocks, there were pockets of slower water. I concentrated on these places and began to see the fish. Trout only inches from the bank in sunlit water. Trout in the quiet water behind a boulder. A dark flash of motion racing up a shallow riffle. Eventually I took a trout—a small brown—on a caddis.

There were no insects hatching. Perhaps it was the time of day, the late runoff, the temperature of the water, the heat of the day, the angle of the sun. No trout rose. Still, I fished a dry fly, more out of hope and habit than reason. I moved fast, a cast or two into each likely spot and then on to the next. My dog Cera, a young golden retriever we had rescued from the pound, raced through the woods along the trail. When I stopped to fish she rested on the bank and watched instead of plunging into the best part of the pool as she sometimes did. Together, we fished up the stream for perhaps a mile. I took three more trout: another small brown and two Rio Grande cutthroats.

Both cutthroats came out of deep shaded pockets formed where fallen timber blocked the flow of the stream. The second was nearly a foot long. It was a beautiful deep-bodied fish with bright red sides, a "red-bellied native" as Elliot Barker would say. I knelt on a high bank, dapping my fly on the dark surface and saw the trout rise to the fly from its shaded home beneath a brush pile, red sides clearly visible. It held inches beneath the fly, watching and waiting, and then faded back into the depths without taking the fly. I lifted the fly from the water, waited a moment and then dapped it again. There was a splash and the trout was on. It thrashed on the surface and dove into the depths of the pocket seeking the shelter of the drowned branches before I lifted it to the bank. I was sorry that I had forgotten to bring my camera because the fish was so lovely and there were small white wildflowers on the green bank that would have made a fine background for a photo. For a moment I looked at the trout, trying to hold the picture in my mind. Then I released it and walked back toward the mesa.

\* \* \*

## JULY 24, 1994

I had reached a point where I was spending so much time working and trying to complete a book that I had forgotten the feeling that made me want to write it. So I did what I usually do when I am feeling out of balance and unfocused. I went fishing. I got up before 5:00 on a Sunday morning, put Cera and my fishing rod and day pack in the car and drove to Borrego Mesa. The roads were empty. I made it in less than an hour, before the sun had risen over the Sangre de Cristos. There was one car at the trailhead, but other than that, the campground was deserted.

When I reached the Rio Medio, it was running clear beneath a canopy of pine and fir and cottonwood. I wanted solitude, and I wanted to catch cutthroats. I thought my chances of finding both would be better a few miles upstream, so I began to walk up the trail that ran beside the river. Cera ranged ahead. The trail ran beneath huge trees and through small meadows. In the meadows there were tall yellow flowers, purple flowers with thin delicate petals shaped like tendrils, tiny white flowers, scarlet paintbrush, and black-eyed susans.

Suddenly I heard a beating of wings and birdcalls and Cera crashing through the brush. Three grouse flushed and flew into the branches of a huge Douglas fir. Cera pranced around the base of the tree, her tail held high, looking up into the branches. She was very excited. I walked over to her and looked up into the tree, searching the dark spidery branches until I saw the plump round forms of the birds. We watched the grouse in the tree and then continued up the stream. Moments later the scene repeated itself, and, as the day wore on, it happened again and again. The woods were filled with grouse. Before we left the canyon, I had seen at least a dozen and heard many more. Each time, Cera flushed the birds from low cover. Each time I heard the beating of their wings and their wild cries. And each time they flew into the high branches of the great trees that grew along the canyon floor.

After walking up the canyon for half an hour, I left the trail and made my way through a thicket of young firs to the river. Just upstream the river made a sharp bend and then flowed toward me beneath the trees in a narrow cobbled run. I began to fish. On my first cast, I hung my fly in a tree and lost it. I tied on a new fly and cast again. A ten inch brown rose up through the glassy water and took the fly. I tightened and the trout leapt into the air, raced over the pale bottom of the stream, and jumped twice more before it tired. The trout was sleek and fine-spotted. I released it and continued up the stream.

The river throbbed with life. Midges hovered above the surface, and small pale moths fluttered along the stream. Caddis flies rose and fell above the riffles and butterflies moved from flower to flower in the meadows. Once I saw a hummingbird, darting low above the surface of the stream. The water was very clear, and the holding spots for trout—small pools, sheltered pockets, and foot-deep runs—were plainly visible.

And the trout were there. Ten minutes after I had released the first fish, another rose from a dark pocket in the lee of a boulder and nailed the fly. In the early morning shadows, I did not see the rise so much as sense it. The trout fought hard, but it was not a large fish. As it came to me I could see that it was a cutthroat about the same size as the brown I had taken earlier. The fish was very heavy for its length. It had a pale golden back, rose-tinted sides, and crimson gill slashes. The spots on the trout's back were sparse, but they ran the length of its body like the spots on a rainbow trout. It looked quite different from the cutthroats I had taken in the Jemez a few weeks earlier, so I snapped a quick photograph of the fish as it lay in the shallows and then I released it. For a moment, the trout held above the pebbled bottom by the bank. Then it slowly finned into deeper water and disappeared.

I walked upstream for another twenty minutes, took off my hiking boots and put on a pair of Teva sandals. I put the boots into the pack and stepped into the stream. The water was cold but not painfully so. It felt good on my tired feet and the muscles of my calves, and for a few moments I just stood in the stream and felt the rush of the current. Then, wading wet, I began to fish again.

As I fished, the sun rose over the ridge, and narrow shafts of sunlight penetrated the forest canopy. Where the sun shone the water glowed, but for the most part, the Rio Medio still ran in shadow. Trout were everywhere. I caught two tiny fish, a brown and a cutthroat, both no more than four inches long, but the rest—a dozen browns and four cutthroats—were all ten inches or better and several of the browns were longer than a foot.

After losing a deer hair caddis in the branches of an overhanging fir tree, I searched my fly box for something that would look enticing to the fish. I settled on a small hopper pattern with a pale deer-hair head and wing that seemed to me to be about the same size and color as the moths that flew just above the surface of the stream. I tied on the hopper and cast it into the run just upstream. The buoyant deer hair fly danced down the broken surface of the run unmolested.

I cast again. This time I did not see the fly at all. But something, perhaps an out-of-place ripple or splash, made me tighten on the line. When I did, I felt a solid throbbing weight. The fish held for a second in the current, shaking its head. Then it raced downstream, angled across the stream and jumped. It was a cutthroat. The trout made another short run and then tired. When I reached down to lift it, the trout was so thick around the body that I could barely get my hand around it. It was nearly fourteen inches long.

Fourteen inches may not sound like much of a trout if you limit your fishing to tailwater fish factories like the San Juan, but in most rivers and especially in a miniature trout stream like the Rio Medio it is one hell of a fish. I once read that the cutthroats in the Rio Medio average ten to fourteen inches. Fish have a way of growing in print. Divide those figures by two and you'll be closer to the truth. Be that as it may, the big cutthroat was the best I have taken in the Rio Medio. It really was *nearly* fourteen inches long, and catching it was the perfect end to a perfect day of fishing.

\* \* \*

A month later I fished the Rio Medio again on a Friday evening after work. It was a foolish thing to do. My wife and the boys were out of town and would be returning the next day. I wanted to leave the office early and get in a few hours of fishing before they returned, but it turned out to be a case of trying to fit a square peg into a round hole. After a hot and hectic day spent trying to finish the things I needed to do, I finally managed to leave the office shortly before 5:00. It was after 6:00 when I parked at Borrego Mesa and nearly 6:30 in the evening by the time I put on my Tevas and slipped into the stream.

The Rio Medio was not the same river I had fished earlier that summer. Dead trees were everywhere. They lay along the banks and across the stream. Their branches trailed in the water and snagged my fly again and again. The water was low and shallow. Pools and runs that had been so inviting not long ago seemed small and exposed. There was nowhere for the trout to hide and not a fish to be seen. The air was cooling and I waited for insects to appear, dancing above the water in the long evening shadows. There were no insects. I looked for rising fish. There were none. I looked at my watch. It was after 7:00. Another hour. That was all the time that was left.

Climbing over the trunk of a fallen Douglas fir I slipped and banged my shin against a broken branch raising a long angry welt.

*Cutthroat water, Sangre de Cristo Mountains*

*Rio Grande Cutthroat Trout, Sangre de Cristo Mountains*

*Rio Grande Cutthroat Trout, Jemez Mountains*

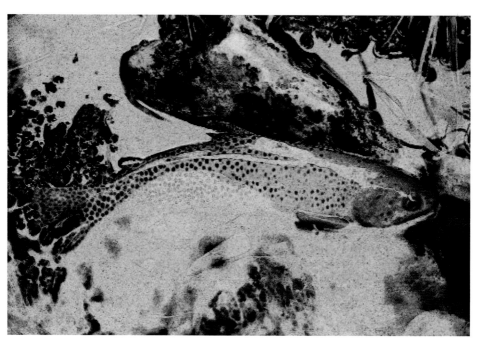

*Rio Grande Cutbow, Sangre de Cristo Mountains*

*Colorado River Cutthroat Trout, San Juan Mountains*

*Brook Trout, Rio de los Pinos*

*Rio Grande Cutthroat Trout, Sangre de Cristo Mountains*

*Cutthroat water, Jemez Mountains*

After the pain subsided I slipped into the stream . . . and stubbed my toe on a rock. Thunder rumbled. I looked at my watch. 7:30. It was hard to decide whether there was too little time left or too much. Too little to catch a trout, but enough to lose two more flies in the branches and cut my ankle on a protruding root. The thunder came again. Night was falling. It was a long way back to the car. There was no time. The tension I had felt at the office remained. I turned and began walking down the river.

* * *

There are countless children's books about magic kingdoms: *Through the Looking Glass, The Lion, the Witch and the Wardrobe,* and *The Indian in the Cupboard* to name just a few. To reach the magic kingdom, you must cross a threshold, some barrier that appears ordinary to others but is a gateway to a place where wonders abound, extraordinary events are the norm and life is lived in the present. The small rivers where trout are found are my magic kingdom, my secret refuge. In this, I think, I am hardly unique, but I still consider myself very fortunate. Most adults have no such place, except perhaps in their memories of childhood.

The magic kingdoms of childhood are the places where the line between imagination and reality blurs. I remember some of them. The rocky outcropping in the park across the street from my home was a fort where battles were lost and won. The cliff at the foot of my bed where tiny painted Indians always defeated the cavalry. The chair in the corner of my room where I read and was transported to other worlds until I felt my mother's hand on my shoulder and heard her voice telling me that it was time for dinner. The magic kingdom of the river is very different from these places. It is real.

On some rivers, the threshold to the magic kingdom is purely internal. I park the car, walk a few dozen feet, and I am at the water's edge. I watch the water, searching for insects and signs of life beneath the surface. I hear a sound, a change in the pitch of the river, a splash or something undefinable. A moment later I hear it again. There! By the far bank, a rise. I watch. The fish rises again. I follow it down beneath the surface as it descends. I watch as it rests, a dark shadowy form hovering just above the pale bottom. The car and the road just a few feet behind me are no longer part of my world. I am there.

On the Rio Medio and on other streams that flow along canyon bottoms, the barrier between the outside world and the magic kingdom of the river is also physical. The top of the mesa and the canyon floor are different worlds. On top there are broad vistas. Between the trees, the ground is dry. The wind blows. The canyon stretches below me, secret and inviting. The descent from the mesa is steep. As I walk down, the trees change. The ground grows wetter. The smells of cottonwood and damp earth rise up along with the sound of the moving water. The canyon walls enfold me. The wind diminishes and then is gone. Everything—sound, sight, and smell, even gravity—draws me down to the river.

There are days when I never cross the threshold into the magic kingdom. I cannot leave the office behind me. My steps are clumsy and my casting inept. I see trout only after I have spooked them. I have no faith in the fly on the end of my leader. But there are others, like the day that Cera flushed covey after covey of grouse on the Rio Medio, when I seem to live there. On those days my senses are heightened. Colors are more vivid. Sounds are clearer and more distinct. The smells of trees and flowers fill my nostrils. Trout rest in every sheltered lie and feed in the riffles. My casts snake through the branches. My shadow never falls on the water. I feel the flow of the current. I am awake.

It is, of course, possible to catch trout without being awake. Anyone who has fished for very long has had the experience of standing in a stream, lost in a daydream or thinking about a problem at the office, with a fly trailing in the water. Suddenly you are awakened by the sharp tug of a trout. It is not supposed to happen that way, but it does. The trout on the end of your line is urgent and alive, and it pulls you back into the present. It is hard to think about a deadline when there is a trout on the other end of your line. The trout is an emissary from the magic kingdom, calling you to return.

Trout are uniquely suited to such a role. In the river they are swift and secret creatures, hiding in the shade of an overhanging bank or lost beneath the broken surface of a riffle. When you catch a glimpse of them in their watery world, they are dark and quick. They blend into the rocks along the bed of the stream. Their colors appear drab and nondescript. But removed from the water, they are often so brightly colored that they hardly seem real. On the wall above my desk there is a photograph of a cutthroat I caught last summer, a black-spotted fish with crimson gill covers, pale gold body, iridescent and barred with faint blue-green parr marks, and a deep orange belly. It is a creature from another world.

The world of the river is forever elusive, forever a mystery. No matter how hard I look into the waters, I never really know them. They change with the spring runoff. They change with the rain. They change when the sun beats down. No two days, or even hours, are ever the same. When I fish a pool where I have always caught fish before and no trout rises to my fly, is it because the pool is barren? Or has some large and cautious old trout driven out, or eaten, all the other fish? Have I engaged in some form of clumsiness known to the trout but not to me? Or is it the angle of the sun, the barometric pressure, or a hatch that ended five minutes before I arrived, leaving the trout too glutted to bother with the feeble imitation tied to my leader? I will never know. Every river is a world of infinite complexity. There is always more to learn and every bit of knowledge reveals a new mystery.

The river is also a place of memories. The big trout that broke off two years ago in the pool that is just around the bend. The fly that worked so well a month ago. The overhanging rock where I took shelter from the rain. Opening day with my father on a drizzly April morning, sitting on a rock just talking. Being alone. Smelling the water. Listening to the river. Moving cautiously along the bank. Hunting fish. A time longer ago than I can remember.

Memory, mystery, and magic fish. The river holds them all. When I open my eyes, they are all there. On my worst day on the Rio Medio, I was walking back toward the mesa. Night was falling. Clouds filled the sky. Thunder rumbled. The stream was too low. The brush was impenetrable. My thoughts were far away. And then the woods along the trail gave way to a small open flat of pale rocks and the path to the river was clear. It was the witching hour. The broken surface of the water was black and copper and glistening.

I cast to a dark pocket in the shallow rocky stream where I knew with absolute certainty that a trout must lie. It was a long cast. The line snaked through the opening in the trees, across the rocks toward the river. For an instant it hung in the air, a pale thread, reaching for the river. The fly landed on the darkening water. A trout rocketed into the air. Again and again. And then it was gone. The dark forms of the trees rose around me. I heard the sound of the river. The air was filled with the smell of night. It was a moment of such beauty that I forgot the cut on my ankle, the climb ahead, everything.

*Chapter Eight*

# Rio Santa Barbara

**JULY, 1990**

I had wanted to fish the Santa Barbara for a long time. The stream was said to hold Rio Grande cutthroat trout. That was reason enough. Even though it was only an hour's drive from my home, I had not fished the Santa Barbara since moving to New Mexico five years earlier. I had only seen the stream once, when I first visited the state two years before moving here. It was October. A friend in Taos had suggested it as a good place to fish. When I got there a heavy wet snow was falling. The upper campground was deserted. I parked and began walking up the stream. The Santa Barbara seemed a very small stream, rushing between snow-covered banks under towering trees. The sky grew darker and the snow fell harder. My breath rose in small clouds. It was no place to be in an old car with rear wheel drive and tires that had seen better days. I turned and followed the stream back to the car.

Seven years later I came back. The years after Danny's birth had been filled with caring for an infant, work, new friends, Adam's little league games and chess tournaments, and a thousand other things. For the first time since I went to college, fishing fell by the wayside. But it never really left my mind. I fished less but thought about it more. I read about the old days and developed a romantic attachment to Rio Grande cutthroat trout. Information was hard to come by, but all indications were that the Rio Santa Barbara was the place to go to catch cutthroats. So you could say that I had been thinking about a trip to the Santa Barbara for a long while.

When the time came, I carefully scrutinized the National Forest map, read what there was to read about the river, which wasn't much, and spent a couple of lunch hours at the fly shop pumping Mark and Jan and any stray patrons who seemed to be in the know for information. And I developed a plan. I would leave home very early on a Saturday morning and be at the trailhead by first light. Then I would hike up the stream for two miles until I got to the first fork. From there I would follow the trail up the Middle Fork for another mile or so and then begin fishing. If there were Rio Grande cutthroats in the Santa Barbara, I felt sure I would find them there.

Like many another meticulously conceived plan, this one did not come off without a few hitches. On Friday night we got a sitter and went out to dinner with our friends Matt and Sue. Mexican food, fajitas with peppers, salsa and onions—lots of onions—washed down with cold Mexican beer. When we got home I packed my fishing gear: my little fly rod, a box of flies, a spool of 4X tippet and some floatant, and a day pack with a sweater, rain jacket, emergency stuff, lunch, and my camera. While my wife readied herself for bed I looked at the Forest Service map again, following the thin line of trail up beyond the first fork to the place I planned to fish.

Sleep did not come. I lay awake and worried. About money, the boys, my old car, my wife's newer car, the roof, the dog, a deadline at work. Time passed. It was after midnight. My wife slept. Calm down, I told myself. You've been looking forward to this trip a long time. Just take it easy and go to sleep. It didn't work. Time passed. I tried sleeping on the sofa. No dice. The bills grew larger. My salary grew smaller. The tapping noise in third gear grew ever more ominous. At 2:00 a.m. I got up to get a drink of water. It was then I remembered the onions. Actually, it might be more accurate to say that they reminded me. Forcefully. My father had brought a saying with him when he came to this country, something about the relationship between onions and sleepless nights. I tried without success to remember how it went. It didn't matter. It was the thought that counted. I understood the source of all my troubles. I crawled back into bed and closed my eyes. The alarm rang. I shut it off and went back to sleep.

When I awoke again it was starting to get light. The alarm clock said it was nearly 6:00 a.m. I jumped out of bed and threw on my clothes. While coffee was brewing I studied the map again. I would be able to fish anywhere along the Middle Fork of the Santa Barbara. The trail followed the stream all the way. When the coffee was done I filled a mug and went out to the car. Then I called my dog Cera. It was going to be her first fishing trip. I was curious to see what kind of a fishing companion she would make.

Cera's approach to getting in the car should have alerted me to the problem. She eyed the old blue Datsun balefully and refused to get in, even when I tried to bribe her with a dog biscuit. Eventually, I half-pulled and half-lifted her into the car, and away we went. As we drove through the empty streets on our way out of Santa Fe, I caught glimpses of Cera in the rearview mirror. She did not look happy.

After leaving Santa Fe we took the high road to Taos. The road wound north through the foothills of the Sangre de Cristos. The mountains were shrouded in clouds. The road passed through sculpted high desert country with eroded rock formations and scattered piñons and junipers. It passed through forests of ponderosa pine. It passed through green meadows and old villages that could have been in another country except for the Ford and Chevy pickup trucks parked beside the old adobe houses and newer trailers. There was a dump just south of Truchas. When we reached it there was garbage strewn along both sides of the road and I had to steer between bits of trash on the roadway.

As we drove down out of Truchas it happened. I heard a shuffling in the back seat, then a gurgling and then silence. A foul smell filled the car. I pulled over. There was a baleful guilty look on Cera's face. Her half-digested breakfast lay on the back seat. The old Datsun's seats were upholstered with slick blue vinyl. It was hot and clammy in summer and stiff and slippery in the winter. They were about as uncomfortable as seats can get. But in that moment of crisis I discovered they had a great virtue. The vinyl was absolutely impermeable and easy to clean. The car's trunk was filled with tools, belts, hoses, and rags, the kind of stuff that keeps an old car running. I wiped off the seat with a handful of rags and stuffed the rags in a torn green trash bag that had also found its way into the trunk. After walking Cera along the roadside for a few minutes, I got her back in the car and we were on our way. With all the windows open.

After passing through Peñasco, we drove up into Santa Barbara Canyon. The road turned to gravel and rose steadily into the mountains. Clouds hung low, obscuring the peaks. Shortly before 8:00 a.m., I parked at the trailhead in the upper campground. It was a big campground, and it was nearly full. But on this overcast morning, many of the campers had slept in. Smoke rose from a few fires. Cera was very happy to get out of the car. I assembled my rod, put on my pack, and started up the trail.

It was wet, a black mud path through the forest. There were horse tracks dug deep into the soft earth. The ferns and other vegetation along the trail were dripping. I wondered if it had rained in the night. Cera raced ahead. Her lower legs were dark with mud. The trail rose and passed through a stand of aspens. Their trunks were tall, slim, and white. The forest floor beneath them was carpeted with lush green grass and scattered wildflowers. The air was cool and moist from the low-hanging clouds.

The trail descended and came down to the Rio Santa Barbara. I had not paid that much attention to the stream while I was driving. In my mind, it was the little stream that I had seen on that snowy fall day a long time ago. To my surprise, it was a pretty good-sized creek, at least for New Mexico. It rushed down through a forest of Douglas firs and aspens. The water was moving very fast, and there were few pools or pockets. I wondered how I would fish it. Thick stands of willow grew along the banks. The ground was carpeted with ferns and grasses. In the openings between the trees and in small meadows, wildflowers dotted the ground, their colors muted in the morning light. Daisies, black-eyed Susans, blue flax, mallows, wild roses, purple asters, and scarlet paintbrush.

I made a few sporadic attempts at fishing as I followed the stream up into the mountains. Once a trout came up to look at my fly, but before the fish could hit it, the current pulled the fly out of the tiny pocket where the trout had risen. A cutthroat? It was impossible to tell. I cast again but the trout did not return. A half mile farther upstream, a trout popped out from behind a rock and nailed the fly. For a second I held my breath. Then I saw the fish. It was a small brown. Are there really cutthroats here at all, I wondered. I released the trout and continued up the stream.

A short while later, a small bridge crossed the stream. The trees along the trail were tall and dark. Steep rock walls rose above the trees. The trail followed the Santa Barbara up into the mountains. A mile after crossing the bridge I came to a fork in the trail. I stopped and pulled the Forest Service map out of my pack. According to the map, Trail 24 followed the Middle Fork which was the branch of the Santa Barbara I wanted to fish. Trail 25 followed the West Branch. I turned left onto Trail 24.

Trail 24 wound up the side of the mountain in a series of long switchbacks. It had not seen much traffic lately. The only tracks were those of a mule deer that had followed the trail for a long way up the mountain before turning off into the trees. Eventually the trail stopped climbing, straightened and followed the side of the mountain. Somewhere down below, the Middle Fork ran between steep forested slopes. I could not see it. The stream seemed very far away. I walked and waited for the trail to descend to the water. An hour after I started up the mountain, the truth finally dawned on me. Trail 24 did follow the Middle Fork . . . four or five hundred feet above the water. I stopped and pulled out the map and looked at it again. On the map, Trail 24 followed the bank of the Middle Fork. But only on the map. I turned and walked back down the mountain.

Shortly before reaching the junction of the two trails, I noticed an unmarked path descending toward the Middle Fork. I turned off Trail 24 and followed the path down across an open hillside of tall grass and flowers to the stream. Cera raced ahead. Near the water the ground was covered with small boulders, smooth round river rocks, and downed timber, much of it rotten. Elk tracks and droppings were everywhere. The willows along the bank were thick. Cera was standing in the icy water, drinking greedily. When she finished, I gave her some dog biscuits and she settled down along the bank to eat and watch.

The Middle Fork was much smaller than the main Santa Barbara but no less swift. The water rushed over the rocks. I had never fished such a fast stream. I cast upstream. The fly landed. The current caught the line and pulled the fly across the stream leaving a wake like a little boat. No trout rose. I wondered again if there really were cutthroats in the Santa Barbara or how I would ever catch anything in the rushing current. For the first time I looked at my watch. It was eleven o'clock.

I ate lunch sitting on the trunk of a fallen tree on the edge of a small meadow along the bank of the stream. It was not much of a lunch; just a peanut butter and honey sandwich, some trail mix and an apple, but I was hungry and tired and it felt very good to sit and eat. While I ate, the sun broke through the clouds. Cera dozed. In the meadow tall yellow flowers rose above the knee-high grass. Small butterflies flitted from flower to flower. The butterflies had intricately patterned wings of black and orange. There were bees at work in the meadow too. I sat and watched them for several minutes. They were oblivious to me.

After finishing lunch I took my camera out of the pack and walked out into the meadow. When I approached, the butterflies flew away. I stood still. One returned. I leaned forward to get close enough to take its picture. My shadow fell on the butterfly and before I could focus the camera, it flew away. I made my way slowly to the next patch of flowers. A butterfly sat on the head of a yellow flower. Its wings were extended. After making sure that the sun was not behind me, I bent towards it, moving as slowly as I could. The butterfly fluttered its wings, but it did not leave its perch on the flower. I focused the camera and pressed the shutter.

For the next half hour I moved through the meadow stalking butterflies. When I was silent and moved very slowly, the insects would let me approach. If I stood motionless, they would ignore me. But when I made a sudden movement, they would fly away across the meadow. I found that if I watched the butterflies very carefully, I could tell when they would let me move closer and when moving nearer would make them fly away. It was not an articulate thing, a particular wing movement, motion of the antennae, or anything else I can name. It was just a kind of tension, or maybe intuition. Not now. Be still. Wait. And now move closer. The sun was warm and the air was still. I could hear the bees buzzing in the meadow above the rush of the stream.

Watchfulness is a habit to which we are not much accustomed. For most of us, constant activity is a central theme of our lives. We are expected to plunge into things and batter them into submission in a whirl of motion. Sometimes, I have the feeling that the world values sound and fury above all. Watchfulness is not rewarded. But constant motion does not always equate itself with results. And patience and close concentration are rightly counted as virtues. Years ago I used to visit a salt flat at low tide to watch blue herons stalk their prey in the shallows. Now the flat is empty. The herons are gone, but the image of the herons hunting remains. The great bird stands motionless in the shallows. For a long while it watches the water waiting for some hapless minnow to come within range. Then it strikes. It seldom misses. After swallowing its prey, the heron resumes its watch. If it moves, it moves very slowly and takes care not to disturb the water.

After I had taken a dozen photographs of butterflies, I put away my camera, picked up my rod, and returned to the river. Cera pranced ahead, her tail waving like a flag. I motioned for her to sit and she sat and watched the water expectantly. The Santa Barbara still raced foaming over the slick round rocks in its bed, but it was a different river. Where before I had seen only rushing water, now I saw small pockets in the current and holding lies along the bank. Where before I had seen branches that reached out to snag my fly, now I saw shelter from predators and shade from the hot afternoon sun. So I began to fish.

Twenty feet downstream, a low hanging willow branch trailed in the swift water. Just upstream, along the bank, there was a run of deeper water. I shook loose some line and flicked the fly downstream. The fly drifted down toward the trailing branch. It vanished in a burst of silver spray. A fish rocketed across the stream, darted back and forth in the current and then tired. I lifted it from the water. It was a trout with a dark back, sides of gold and orange and red shaded by parr marks, black spots clustered toward its tail and crimson slashes beneath its lower jaw. It was not a big trout, but it was deep-bodied and beautiful, and it was a cutthroat. I killed the fish and put it in my creel on a bed of ferns I found growing along the bank.

For two hours I fished up the Middle Fork. Along the banks the ground was rough and uneven. Fallen trees blocked my way. The rocks in the stream bed were round and slick. It was slow going, but there were fish in the river. In a deep pocket below a boulder near the far bank, a trout rose and inhaled my fly before the current could pull it from the slack water. I knew before seeing the fish that it was a cutthroat. In that perfect pocket in the rushing water what else could it be? I was wrong. The trout was a ten-inch brown. I released it.

There were cutthroats in the canyon. I caught two small ones in quick runs along the bank of the stream. They were fish as fast as the water rushing down from the heart of the Pecos and as lovely as the sparkling stream. They belonged in the river. I released them.

Eventually I came to a spot where a fallen tree lay halfway across the stream, forming a small dam and diverting most of the stream's flow towards the far bank. Below the fallen tree there was a small pool. The pool was clear except in one corner where water spilled over the tree trunk and the surface was flecked with foam. I cast into the glassy water. Twice. Nothing happened. The fly drifted aimlessly in the still water before the current pulled it from the pool. Out of the corner of my eye I saw a dimple in the foam. I cast. The fly landed and vanished. I struck. A fish jumped. A good one. The fight was dogged, but the trout was well hooked, and in the little river, it never had a chance. A minute later a fine brown trout lay on the bank. I decided to keep it for dinner.

I continued working up the stream. In a run of quick water along a rocky wall I took another cutthroat. I released it. On the next cast I put the fly high into the willows. The fly was solidly lodged in a high branch, far beyond my reach, so I broke it off. After tying on a deer hair caddis, I looked at my watch. It was nearly two o'clock. Time to start back. I left the stream and made my way back through the woods toward the trail. It was hard going, but in a short while I came to the path that had taken me down to the Middle Fork. I followed it through fields of tall green grass where butterflies moved among yellow flowers. Elk tracks and droppings were everywhere. Before reaching the main trail, I stopped to take more photographs of butterflies.

When I reached Trail 24 I began walking faster. Thunder rumbled in the mountains behind me. I had it in mind to continue straight back to the parking area. But the Santa Barbara was running in the canyon beneath the trail and there were pockets and runs that looked like they had to hold fish. It was hard to look at the water and pass by. Too hard for me. After ten minutes of walking, I cut down a steep wooded slope to the stream and began to fish. The water was even faster here and the stream was larger. Twice trout rose up out of the fast water, flashed at the fly, and vanished.

The banks were steep and choked with brush and fallen timber. It was easier to walk down through the shallow water along the edge of the stream. The rocks in the streambed were round and slick. My hiking boots were soon soaked. The icy water felt good on my feet and ankles. I made my way down the stream until I came to a log jam where the current had pushed dead wood up against a row of dark boulders. The water along the logjam was deep and fast. I watched the surface. A few caddis flies danced above the water. They were smaller and darker than the fly on my leader. Inches from the tangle of branches and tree trunks I thought I saw the dimple of a rise in the black swift water. There were bubbles on the surface of the rushing stream. I wondered if what I had seen was a fish. A minute later, there was another dimple, tiny like the first. I cast. The fly drifted along the edge of the logjam, a speck in the foaming current. It disappeared in a dimple. The fish was on. It was strong and fast. And it was very lovely. I took a photograph of the trout as it lay on the gray pebbles beside the Santa Barbara. It was a cutthroat, shaped like a football, with a dark back and golden red-orange sides. Its photograph is on the wall above my desk. After taking its picture, I killed the trout and put it in my creel. That was more than a dozen years ago. It was the last Rio Grande cutthroat I ever kept.

The storm was drawing nearer. Thunder rolled. A gust of cold air blew down the canyon. I cleaned the fish in the creel and then scrambled up the hillside to the trail. Cera ranged ahead. Rain began to fall. I walked faster. Lightning flashed. The clouds were low and dark and I could feel the wind. I was half jogging, hoping to reach the car before the storm. And then the storm was upon us. Big drops of rain splatted down. Hail followed. Trees swayed in the wind. Lightning bounced along the ridges. Thunder shook the ground. The car was still a half-mile away. By the time I reached it, I was soaked to the skin and Cera's legs and belly were black with mud. She crawled into the back seat of the Datsun and was half asleep by the time I finished putting my gear in the trunk.

## AUGUST, 1994

I woke in the night to the sound of rain drumming on the roof. When I woke again, the rain had stopped. I turned off the alarm and got out of bed. Then I went to the kitchen where I ate a bowl of cereal. After eating, I went out to the car, which I had packed the night before. It was dark. There were no stars. Clouds filled the sky. I could not see the ridge of the mountains. For a moment I hesitated, wondering whether I should go at all. To reach the stream I would have to drive for an hour and walk two more. Putting in the effort to fish a new stretch of stream that holds native cutthroats was one thing. Putting it in to get rained on was another. Then to the north I saw a slice of sky open in the cloud cover and then another. I called Cera and we were off.

The roads were empty and I made good time. As I drove it grew light. More spaces opened between the clouds, but they continued to look dark and ominous and full of rain. I took the low road up through Española and then along the Rio Grande to Embudo where I turned east. The Rio Grande was low and murky. The Rio Embudo, which is normally a rushing stream, was only a trickle in its dry rocky bed. Still, in Dixon where the road crossed an arroyo, a small stream of water ran across the pavement where it was covered by mud and earth that the previous night's thunderstorms had flushed down from the hills above.

After leaving the narrow green valley of the Rio Embudo, the road climbed over a ridge of stark dry hills and then descended into the rich flat valley. I could see the jagged forms of the Truchas Peaks to the south, but the tops of other mountains were obscured by clouds. Shortly after seven o'clock I parked at the trailhead. There were more than a dozen cars parked there. The campground was still sleeping.

The black earth of the trail that led up the Rio Santa Barbara was wet and soft. There were no footprints or tracks. The rain had washed the trail clean. The air was cold and wet. The shrubs along the trail were dripping. It had been two years since I had walked this trail and the aspens seemed to have grown and there were more than I remembered. Many had names and dates carved in their bark. Against the dark Douglas firs, the aspens were very pale and spare. Their white trunks seemed to give off a kind of light, illuminating the forest.

Despite the rain that had fallen, the Santa Barbara was very low. The water was swift and shallow. Fishable pockets and pools were few and far between. The West Fork would be even smaller. Cera ranged through the woods looking for grouse and squirrels. Her fur was matted and wet from the dripping underbrush. Her legs were black with mud from the trail. Steep rocky outcroppings rose above the Douglas firs. Heavy clouds filled the sky. The woods were dark and quiet. Drops of water glistened on a spider web beside the trail. The air was still. I heard the rhythmic sounds of my breathing and footfalls on the trail above the rush of the stream. Forty minutes after leaving the campground, I came to a fork in the trail. I took the West Fork Trail and descended to the stream. Picking my way from rock to rock I crossed the Santa Barbara and then followed the West Fork Trail up through the woods.

The trail soon veered away from the stream. In a small clearing, I passed a couple sitting on a stump by their tent. They sat silently, smoking, and seemingly lost in thought. We did not speak. Then they were behind me, and I was alone in the woods. Clouds filled the sky, low and heavy and pregnant with electricity and violence. The air was still. The only sounds were my breathing and my footfalls. Then I heard the sound of running water and saw the West Fork in a narrow canyon below me. It was a small and rushing stream. There were no pockets or pools for trout to hide, just shallow tumbling water, hardly worth fishing. Thunder rumbled in the mountains ahead. I thought about turning back, but kept walking.

Fifteen minutes later the character of the stream changed. Its current slowed, and as it wound around a bend, it formed a pool. I left the trail and walked down through a small meadow to the stream. As I approached, a trout dimpled the surface at the tail of the pool. I inched my way toward the water and stood silently watching for it to rise again. A fish rose, but this time by the far bank near the head of the pool. I looked into the stream until my eyes adjusted, and then I saw them. Two trout. A small fish in the slick at the tail of the pool and a larger one in the deep water at its head. They were stocky, black-spotted fish. Neither sensed my presence. They held in the glassy water and periodically rose to pluck some unseen insect from the surface. I dabbed a drop of floatant onto my deer hair caddis and then cast it into the fast water above the pool. The fly bobbed in the current and then floated into the head of the pool. The larger fish rose to inspect it, drifted for a moment beneath the fly and then sucked it in. I tightened and the fish was on. It fought strongly but in the tiny stream there was no place for it to go. A moment later I held it in my hand. It was a cutthroat, thick-bodied and rose-sided. I released it. The trout vanished into the clear water. I watched the empty pool. The sky was dark.

In a short while I came to a place where the stream ran through a small steep-sided canyon. Fallen trees littered the hillsides on both sides of the canyon and lay across the water, blocking its flow and forming a series of pale silt-bottomed pools. Thick brush lined the stream. I followed Cera down into the canyon. The brush was dripping wet. It had rained here the night before. My legs were soaked by the time I made my way through the fallen trees and brush to the stream. The first pool was empty, but in the second, a dark shadow hovered over the bottom beside a sunken log. Cera sat beside me, watching the water intently. Her tail switched back and forth. I cast. The fly drifted past the log. The shadow rose up, metamorphosed into a trout, and took the fly. I felt the fish strong and alive as it raced around the pool, shaking its head and trying to free itself of the hook. And then it was in my hand. A foot-long cutthroat, heavy and sleek, pale as the bottom of the stream with bright red gill slashes, silvery olive sides, and a faint rose blush along its belly. I released the trout and it swam across the silty bottom to the shelter of the log. Then it was gone. The air was still.

I fished up through the fallen timber, took another trout and then returned to the trail. I followed it until it leveled out in a forest of fir and then walked back to the stream. The current was slower now, and the stream wound through the forest in a series of riffles and small pools. The stream was very small, seldom more than ten feet across. At a bend in the narrow channel the current had undercut the bank and formed a deep shaded pocket. A fallen tree lay across the water just above the overhung bank. I approached it slowly. The water was dark and still. The branches of the fallen tree formed a screen over the pocket. There was no way to cast a fly into it. I stood on the bank and looked down into the water. The long dark form of a big cutthroat hovered in the tangle of drowned limbs. I watched the trout. It moved to the side, opened its mouth and then moved back. I wanted the trout badly, but it was safe. There was no way to reach it with a fly and there would be no way to pull it from the safety of the branches. I did not move, but somehow the trout sensed my presence and slid back beneath the bank. A gust of cold wind blew. The sky was dark. Thunder rolled in the distance. The air smelled of rain.

A hundred yards upstream, the stream made a sharp bend to the right against a high overhanging bank, forming a slow deep run. The water was very clear. The bottom was pale, almost white. Low shrubs grew on the bank and overhung the stream. In the run were two trout. They finned slowly in the current. Occasionally one would move to the side or up toward the surface to take in some bit of food. The trout were large fish. They moved slowly and deliberately.

I had my usual deer hair caddis fly on the leader. The trout lived high in the mountains, far from any road. I didn't think that my choice of fly would matter much. I was wrong. I cast. The fly landed two feet above the downstream fish. The trout saw the fly, rose up toward it, stopped a few inches below the surface, and then descended. I waited and cast again. This time the trout did not move. It was not spooked, but the fish knew a fake when it saw one. I took off the caddis and replaced it with a small floating black ant.

Then I cast again. When the ant hit the water, the upstream fish turned, swam down to the fly and gently inhaled it. As the trout descended in the current I tightened the line and felt the weight of the fish and saw its side flash in the clear water as it bored for the tangle of roots beneath the undercut bank. It never reached them. I turned the trout, and a moment later it lay half out of the water on the pale gravel beside the stream. It was a beautiful fish, thick-bodied, brightly colored and iridescent. Its sides were deep orange-rose. Its back was a greenish brown with a silvery sheen. The cutthroat slashes beneath its gills were bright crimson. Large black spots clustered near its tail. I freed the hook from its lip and released it. The trout held in the lee of a small rock, gathering strength. Then, with a sudden movement, it swam into the hidden water beneath the undercut bank and disappeared. The run was empty. Limpid water flowed across the white streambed. Thunder rumbled. Cera whimpered and moved close to me. The first raindrops fell.

We took shelter beneath a tree and waited for the rain to pass. The sky was now a solid mass of clouds. The clouds hung low and hid the ridge-tops. It grew dark, and the rain fell harder. I stood beneath the tree and watched the raindrops dimpling the surface of the stream. The air was cold. The rain continued. Small puddles formed along the faint trail that followed the bank of the stream. The rain beat down, fracturing the mirrored surface of the stream and hiding the world beneath. The spell was broken. I put on my pancho and began the long walk to the car.

*Chapter Nine*

# THE MONSTER

There is an old saying that "all fishermen are liars except you and me, and sometimes I'm not so sure about you." I once remarked in passing to another fisherman that I had caught a couple of native cutthroats better than twelve inches in a certain small stream. He was impressed. "I've fished there lots of times," he told me, "and I've never seen a cutthroat bigger than ten inches." The fisherman in question had written an article on that particular stream in which he stated that the cutthroats averaged twelve to fourteen inches. I kept my mouth shut.

It gets worse. A couple of years ago a story was circulating about a local fisherman who caught and released a twenty-seven-inch rainbow on a dry fly in a tributary of the Rio Grande. Like most fish stories, this one had a grain of truth but not much more. The fisherman in question had gone fishing on the tributary. But he didn't catch a twenty-seven-inch rainbow. In fact, he didn't catch any trout at all. He did have one on momentarily—a pretty nice one too; a brown trout about twelve inches long—but it got away. He mentioned the lost brown to his fishing buddy as the highlight of a fishless day, because there were no other fish to mention. His buddy told a friend, and the friend told someone else. It wasn't much of a story, but it got a little more interesting every time it was told. In the space of a week, the trout that got away grew a good fifteen inches, changed species, and got caught.

When it comes to fish stories though, pike fishermen have us trout types beat hands down. They elevate stretching the truth to a high art. Take, for example, the famous Lake Kaiserwag pike. This monstrous fish was supposed to have weighed three hundred and fifty pounds and been nineteen feet long. What it actually was, though, was a hoax, a kind of Piltdown Man of fishes. A number of pike were sectionally mounted and joined to form one huge fish. In the middle ages, pike were reported to attack swans, people, and even mules. There are tales of pike living for more than two hundred years. All of these stories are pure bunk, and help explain why a popular little device for weighing and measuring fish is called a "de-liar". But like most persistent myths, they also have a core of truth. Pike do grow large and they are predators. Their mouths are filled with long needle-sharp teeth. As fish go, they are scary creatures. My guess is that if they lived on land, ranchers would shoot them on sight and they would have long since gone the way of the grizzly bear and the lobo.

\* \* \*

On the Sunday before Thanksgiving I got up before dawn. It was a cool clear morning. I put my fishing gear in the car, called Cera, and began the drive north from Santa Fe. As I drove, the sun rose in a cloudless sky. Two hours after leaving, and after passing through the mining town of Questa, I turned west on a road that led across the mesa to the rim of the Rio Grande Gorge. Snow blanketed the mesa and the conical volcanic mountains that rose on both sides of the river.

After several miles, the road turned south and followed the edge of the Gorge towards the confluence with the Red River. Before reaching it, I turned off on a spur road that led to the trail to Big Arsenic Springs. The road was snowy and rutted. I followed it to the edge of the Gorge. I parked and let out the dog. It was very cold. I cursed myself for not bringing gloves. While Cera ate, I rigged my new fly rod. It was beautiful, a four piece graphite for 5 weight line. It was light, strong, and flexible, and it cast like a dream. After Cera had finished her breakfast and I had polished off a couple of chocolate chip cookies and a final cup of coffee, I put on my pack and we headed down into the Gorge.

The dark basalt walls of the Gorge were dusted with snow. The air was still and cold. I could see the green ribbon of the Rio Grande far below. Twisted piñons and junipers clung to the slopes. There were small birds in the trees. They chattered as the dog raced ahead. My hands ached from the cold. Part way down, I stopped and searched my pack for an extra pair of socks. I found them and put them on like mittens. They helped, but only a little. I put on my pack and continued down. The trail was steep and slippery, a mix of snow and frozen earth. It descended quickly, reached a level shelf where ponderosa pines replaced the piñons and junipers, and then dropped again to the river and Big Arsenic Springs.

The Springs emerged from the foot of the canyon wall where rainwater and melted snow that had percolated down through six hundred feet of porous basalt came up against a layer of impermeable sediment. At the base of the cliffs, clear water burst from the rocks in a wild profusion of green vegetation. The water formed a small stream that flowed over a bottom of lush weeds for a hundred feet before plunging down a short slope of broken basalt to join the Rio Grande. Steam rose where the water from the Springs met the river.

The Springs reminded me of limestone streams I had fished in Pennsylvania. The water was glassy and weeds waved in the current. I wondered if there were trout in the pools of the Springs. In a clear pocket I got my answer. A small brown trout held nervously in the current and then darted away when I approached.

The Rio Grande was high for late fall, and the water had a greenish tinge. In the eddies and backwaters near the bank, a sparse hatch of snowflies played along the surface. They were tiny gray insects, so small that the fly patterns that worked when fish rose to them imitated clusters of the flies rather than a single insect. It was hard to imagine that trout would rise to them, and on this morning none did. It was too cold to expect rising fish. I tied on a double hackle peacock nymph and began making short upstream casts, drifting the fly through the deep pockets along the bank. As I fished, Cera followed me up the river, scrambling over the slick black boulders when I walked and resting in patches of dry grass between the rocks when I stopped to cast.

The fishing was slow. Very slow. After a while I switched to a black wooly bugger. My luck did not improve, but the sun rose over the walls of the Gorge and the day began to warm. I took off my down jacket and stuffed it in my pack. The air in the Gorge was clear and still. I had the river to myself. Snowflies floated on the surface. It seemed like a perfect day to fish, but for two hours I didn't have a strike or see a fish. I worked heavily weighted flies through the deep pockets along the banks where I knew that trout must live. I tried to make the flies act like living things. I waited expectantly for the sharp tug of a trout. It did not come.

Then, in the seam along the slack water formed by a black boulder that jutted out into the current, a trout rose, took something in the current about a foot below the surface, and slid back down into the shadows. I waited a moment and then cast the wooly bugger. The trout hit it immediately. It fought sluggishly and I quickly played it to the shore. The fish was a foot-long brown. It was weak and thin, and it looked like it had already spawned. I released the trout into the still water by the bank. It hovered in the current and then slid back into the green depths beneath the boulder.

The trout renewed my faith in the river. I fished out each cast with intensity and care. Between casts I watched the surface for rising fish. But it made no difference. The trout was an aberration. No fish rose to the snowflies along the banks and none showed any interest in my offerings. It was as if some great force had emptied the river of fish. Clear green water rushed over dark rocks. The sun was warm. My concentration began to lapse. Why fish when there are no fish in the river? I searched the sky above the Gorge looking for eagles. The sky was empty and blue except for the vapor trails of two jets high above. Fishing seemed almost beside the point. I noticed that I was hungry.

After feeding Cera, I ate lunch at a picnic table in a lean-to on a high bank overlooking the river. After lunch I walked back downstream to the Springs. I had not tried fishing where the Springs entered the river, so I decided to circle down below and then work back upstream. Maybe the trout would be more active where the waters from the Springs warmed the icy currents of the river, if there were any trout. It was worth a shot. Nothing else was happening. When I reached the Springs I noticed a small sign. It told me that the vines along the ground were poison ivy. It was the first time I had seen the stuff since moving to New Mexico, but I still had a healthy respect for it. I picked my way carefully through the vegetation to get to the river.

When I reached the bank I looked upstream. The water was shallow and clear where the Springs flowed into the Rio Grande. The current was slow. Farther from the bank the water deepened into a boulder-strewn pool. I watched the shallow water carefully. It looked like a good place for a big trout to rest. The dark forms of rocks were visible along the bottom. A few snowflies drifted across the surface. No trout moved. Nothing. In a foot of water near the shore, there was a sunken log about four feet long. It seemed out of place. I could not recall having seen a log on the bottom of the river before. I looked closer. The log lay still on the bottom. I looked harder, and as I watched, the log took shape.

The log was a pike, long and deep-bodied, with white spotted sides and a head like an alligator. The pike lay motionless in the shallows. It was the biggest fish I had ever seen in fresh water. I looked at my beautiful new fly rod. It seemed to shrink in my hand. I wished for something with more backbone, but it was all I had. I cut back my leader and tied on a 2x tippet. It was the heaviest I had. Normally it looked liked a cable. Now it seemed gossamer thin. Then I searched my streamer fly box for big streamers. The largest I could find was a four-inch-long black leech pattern. For years I had wondered why I even bothered to carry the fly with me. It took up a lot of space in my fly box and had never provoked so much as a follow from a trout although I didn't doubt that it had probably scared a few out of their wits. Now I wondered if it was big enough to interest the pike. I knotted it to the tippet.

The pike was still lying in the shallows facing the shore. I cast the fly upstream of the pike, between the great fish and the bank. The heavily weighted streamer hit the water with a splash. I half expected the pike to flee from the noise, but it did not. I retrieved the slinky black fly as enticingly as I could. The fly darted and danced in the water. The pike did not move. I waited a moment and then cast again. This time the pike came alive. Its fins quivered and it watched the fly intently. It reminded me of all the little pickerel I had caught as a boy in the moment before they darted from the weeds to seize a minnow. The fly passed before the pike. The big streamer looked ludicrously small. The pike's entire body seemed to tense. Still it did not move. The dark slinky fly twitched and wavered in the still water. Suddenly the pike shot forward and took the fly in a rush. I struck. The long five weight rod bent double. The pike paused and then streaked into the deep center of the pool. The reel screamed. Then the pike slowed and moved steadily upstream. I followed.

I put as much pressure on the fish as I dared, but the pike didn't seem to notice. It just moved where it wanted to go. Sometimes it swam up the river taking line from the reel. Sometimes it drifted down with the current. There was nothing I could do to control the fish. And then the line stopped dead. I felt nothing alive, just dead weight. I wondered if the line had snagged on a boulder. I tapped on the rod. It is an old trick. Usually the vibrations make a fish move if it is in the rocks. Nothing happened. I was sure the pike was gone. I felt empty.

I began walking up the bank, following the line upstream, hoping to at least retrieve my fly. And then I saw the pike resting in the shallows facing the bank. It was enormous. The line led from my rod tip toward the pike. I put more pressure on the line just in case the pike was still on. I felt only dead weight. I tapped on the rod. The pike did not move. I was certain now that the pike had left the fly in the rocks, so I approached the great fish to get a closer look. The fish saw me. Its eyes fixed on mine. For a moment we watched each other. I tried to read the look in the pike's eyes. They were empty and cold. I was glad that the pike lived in the river and I lived on the land. Suddenly the pike turned, flicked its tail and glided off into the depths of the pool. The reel sang. The pike was still on.

The fight continued. The pike swam where it wanted. I could not stop it. Sometimes I had the sense that the big fish was tiring, but whenever it came into the shallows and I approached it, the pike would sense my presence and take off into the depths of the pool. When it ran away from me I could see the width of its white-spotted back. I had never seen anything like it. The pike was enormous.

Most of the time I fish in places where there are few big fish. When I fish where there are big fish, they seldom wind up on the end of my line. But on those rare occasions when one does, I can usually work out a plan for landing it on a gravel bar or sandy bank. Not this time and not this fish. It was just too big, and it was a pike, not a trout. I had some seriously mixed feelings about getting my hand within striking distance of a mouth full of long razor sharp teeth. The banks of the river were rocky. The water was very cold. There was no place where I could slide the tired monster into the shallows and beach it. If it ever got tired. The light rod was no match for the fish. Even bent double it seemed to do little more than annoy the pike. Sometimes it didn't even seem to do that. I had the feeling that the pike was ignoring me. My right wrist and forearm ached. I didn't know what to do, so I held on, tried to keep the pike moving and followed it up and down the long pool when it decided to move. Time passed.

And then the line went slack. At first I thought that the pike's teeth had finally cut through the leader, but when I pulled in the line, the fly was still there. The hook had simply pulled out. Maybe it had never penetrated the pike's bony mouth at all. It didn't matter. I was numb. I remembered the time I had lost a huge rainbow on the Conejos. I was angry then. Not now. The pike was just too big. Landing it never seemed real or even possible. I looked into the river searching for the fish. The pool was empty and still. Snowflies floated in the shallows. The pike was gone. I remembered the width of its back. I remembered its weight on the line like a boulder in the river. I remembered its length as it lay in the shallows. I remembered its cold dead eyes.

I sat on the bank and watched the river. Cera sat beside me. After a long while, I began to fish again. In the same pool another very large fish hit the leech as it swung through the slow water between two boulders in midstream. Another pike? I think so, but I will never know. I felt the strike. I felt the weight of the fish. I felt the slow shaking of its head. Then the hook pulled loose. I never saw the fish. I continued to cast for a while, but the pool had gone dead. I decided to fish downstream.

The leech had lost its magic. It moved unmolested through dark fishy pockets and deep pools. I switched to a wooly bugger. The fish were not interested. I took off the wooly bugger and tied on a caddis larva with a split shot and a strike indicator. I fished the little nymph with short upstream casts, watching the orange strike indicator as the fly drifted downstream with the current.

In the Rio Grande, you sometimes come across sand- or mud-bottomed flats with big rocks and boulders where the water is a foot or two deep and the current is slow. They are good places to fish. In one of these spots the strike indicator suddenly darted upstream. I set the hook and a big rainbow thrashed on the surface. The fish fought sluggishly in the cold water. In a few minutes I beached it and tossed it into a snow bank. The trout was a shade over eighteen inches long and shaped like a football. In retrospect it was probably the best rainbow I have ever taken from the Rio Grande. At the time, it didn't move me. Instead, the thought crossed my mind that the trout would have made a nice bait for the big pike.

After dispatching the fish with a rock I cleaned it. The trout was a female filled with eggs. Its stomach was full of a mix of green weeds from the bottom and little green caddis larvae. The insects were a little smaller and brighter green than the size fourteen pattern that the trout had taken, but otherwise, the imitation seemed a pretty good match for the naturals.

After cleaning the fish, I looked at my watch. It was an old digital watch. Sometime during the course of the day it had died. The date and time bore no relationship to reality. They were simply random numbers. I had no idea what time it really was, but the sun was sinking toward the western wall of the Gorge, and it was getting colder, so I hooked the trout on a stick and started up the trail. Cera trotted ahead.

During the day the trail had thawed into a mixture of mud and wet snow. It was soft and slippery. It didn't bother Cera, but for me the six hundred foot ascent to the top of the mesa was a tough, sloppy climb. I wondered what it would have been like carrying a four-foot-long fish. Probably a lot easier.

When I reached the top the sun was beginning to set. The snow-covered Sangre de Cristo mountains in the east were pink in the fading light. The sky was gray and cold. Despite the exertion of the hike up, I was cold. My legs were a little shaky. It felt very good to sit down in the car and turn on the heat. Cera jumped into the back of the car and was asleep in minutes.

The mesa was covered with snow. When I reached the settlement of Cerro, the houses looked lonely and small on the snowy plain. Smoke rose from the chimneys into a darkening sky. The mountains behind them were silent and white. Winter was still a month away.

There would be long cold months ahead. I longed for a warm fire. And for the spring.

When I got home I told my wife and boys about the pike. Adam gave me a hard time about my "fish story." "Sure," he said, "I believe that you lost a fish that was four feet long. I believe you. I really do. Of course I'm just a kid and I still believe in the tooth fairy, so what do I know." They all laughed. But when I said that I wanted to go back to the river with some tackle that might hold the big pike, Adam asked me if he could come too.

# Chapter Ten

## BIG TESUQUE CREEK

Big Tesuque Creek holds a special place in my affections. It is a small steep stream that drains the slopes of Tesuque Peak behind the city of Santa Fe. The trailhead from which the Bear Wallow Trail descends to the creek is only a twenty-minute drive from my home. Big Tesuque Creek was the last place that my wife and I hiked together the winter she was pregnant with our second son. It was the first place I carried Danny in a pack the summer he was born. And it is the closest trout stream to the city.

Danny was born in early April after a difficult pregnancy. He was a restless infant and an early riser. On a Sunday morning eight weeks after his birth, I took him down to Big Tesuque Creek on the Bear Wallow Trail. I was stir crazy from being in the house, Danny was nursing every few hours, and the creek was the only stream close enough to home for me to hike with Danny between feedings. He rode in a pack against my stomach. He was warmly dressed against the morning chill. A light breeze stirred the leaves of the aspens. He smiled at the kaleidoscope of shimmering green above us. He dozed and woke again as the trail descended, followed the stream and then climbed back up the mountain.

It became a ritual that summer. Every Sunday morning I would drive with Danny to the trailhead, hike down to the creek, follow it up the mountain for a mile and then hike back up to the car. It was a special time. He was soft and warm against my body, and he was always very happy. As the summer progressed, Danny dozed less and grabbed for small branches along the trail. But he never stopped smiling at the aspen leaves as they danced overhead. On the way back home I would pick up some danish pastry and *The New York Times*. In the brief hours between Danny's feedings, Big Tesuque Creek met many needs. I got to walk along a trout stream, Danny got his first taste of the woods, and Randy got to sleep late on Sundays.

It has been many years since Danny rode in that pack. Still, when I feel the need to get away and my time is limited, I love to walk the Bear Wallow Trail and follow Big Tesuque Creek. I especially like to go in the early morning. Because of its proximity to town, the trail is a popular hiking spot. I cherish solitude, so I try to get there before other hikers begin to walk.

The Bear Wallow Trail descends to the stream through a forest of mixed conifers interspersed with stands of aspen and small open meadows. Cottonwoods grow near the springs and seeps along the trail. Beneath the tall trees, there are small twisted oaks. A hundred feet above the stream, on an open south-facing slope where no trees obstruct the sun, the forest gives way to a small patch of high desert foliage where yucca and cactus grow. Then the trail curves around the hillside, the forest closes around you, and the sound of running water rises up from below as you make the final descent through the woods to Big Tesuque Creek.

The creek is steep and brushy. It rushes down the hillside over a bottom of rocks, gravel and pale sand. In many places fallen branches and trees dam its flow, creating little pools and waterfalls. The water is always clear and very cold.

No one notices the trout. But if you approach the stream carefully, you can see them, wraiths, grey against the pale bottom. They are incredibly swift and very shy. A quick motion will send them darting into hiding. Most of the trout are small, four to six inches, but if you follow the stream away from the trail, move slowly and approach a deep shaded pocket from below, you may be rewarded by the sight of a ten-inch trout finning in the current waiting for the creek to bring the next meal.

When autumn comes, the creek shrinks and the brown trout spawn in the low clear water. The spawners are the true giants of the creek. Some are nearly a foot long. They rest in pairs, plainly visible, in shallow runs and in the tails of pools. But to see them you must stalk them from below. Despite the spawning urge, they are wild brown trout and they are always vigilant.

Big Tesuque Creek holds both brown trout and rainbows. It is hard to tell the species of small trout in the stream, but almost all of the fish that I have been able to identify have been browns. One trout that I know was not a brown was a fat rainbow that lived in a deep pool above a fallen log. The pool lay beneath a steep bank covered with pine needles. I came upon it on an early fall morning as I walked along the stream. It was shaded by tall ponderosa pines. The water was dark and still. As I approached the pool, a dimple appeared on the surface. I sat down on the high bank and watched. The dimple came again. I scanned the surface for insects but saw none. The fish was feeding on something very small. I broke off a small piece of a twig and tossed it in the pool. The trout rose, inspected the bit of wood and slowly descended. Before it vanished, the trout passed through a patch of sunlit water where I could see it clearly. It had a thick body and fine black spots. A rainbow.

Two weeks later, on a Sunday morning in late October, I came to the stream again. This time I brought my camera with a telephoto lens and polarizing filter, thinking I would capture the rainbow on film. It was not to be. After finishing my morning coffee, I called Cera and made the short drive up the Ski Basin Road. We arrived at the trailhead just before 9:00 a.m. Only one other car was parked there. It was a cool, still morning. The sky was cloudless and deep blue. I stuffed my jacket in the daypack, and we started down the trail toward the creek.

The leaves on the oaks that grew beneath the big trees were reddish-brown. Two weeks earlier the aspens had been in their glory, bright yellow leaves on slim white limbs, trembling against a great expanse of blue sky. Now they were bare. Their round leaves covered the trail, turning grey and brown, looking like two-dimensional stones in the slanting light.

When we reached the creek the water was low and clear. Cera waded into the stream and took a long drink. I felt the water with my finger. It was icy. We crossed the stream and followed the trail down the hillside for several hundred yards before cutting back through the woods to the creek. It was a very small stream, and it was thickly overgrown with willows. It flowed though a maze of fallen timber, splitting and coming together again, forming bathtub-sized pools and narrow channels. The sun had not yet risen above the mountain walls, and the water was in shadow.

I put on a pair of polarized sunglasses and then we began to work our way back up the creek. Cera had drunk her fill and was content to stay well back from the stream. I moved slowly up the bank looking for trout. They were there. Browns waiting to spawn. Almost every pool held fish. They rested in pairs in the tails of the pools and in graveled runs. Some looked surprisingly large, perhaps as long as a foot. It was hard to tell. The creek was so small and shallow that it seemed to magnify the fish. A few of the bigger fish had enlarged heads and the hooked lower jaws that male browns develop when they spawn. Some were mottled. I wondered if they were sick or if it was a color change due to spawning or maybe even some local adaptation.

My eyes grew more and more attuned to the water. Trout hid under tiny grassy banks and under logs. Sometimes I got so close I could see their mouths open as they moved in the current to take in some bit of food. Sometimes a careless footfall sent them darting for cover, leaving the little pools empty and lifeless. Time slowed.

The sun rose above the ridges and shafts of sunlight illuminated the water. For the first time I noticed hikers on the trail. I wondered how many had passed me as I followed the stream that paralleled the trail up the mountain. Fifty feet apart we moved in different worlds.

When we reached the pool where the rainbow had been I sat on the high bank and waited. The water was still in shadow and I saw nothing. After ten minutes I tossed a tiny piece of wood into the water. No fish rose. I waited and then tossed another bit of wood into the stream. It drifted unmolested through the pool. I wondered if the trout had moved out of the pool or been caught. I thought it unlikely that the fish would willingly leave this dark pool and even more unlikely that it had fallen prey to a fisherman. In many years of walking the stream and watching its trout, I had never seen anyone fishing. I watched the pool for a long time, but the rainbow did not appear. Eventually, I had to leave. In later trips to the stream, I looked for the rainbow, but I never saw it again.

I have only fished in Big Tesuque Creek a few times. It is a tough place to fish with a fly rod. The creek is narrow and swift, and it runs beneath a canopy of trees and brush. In many places there are deadfalls and the stream is choked with fallen trees. There is little room along the overgrown banks to cast a fly and little room on the water where a fly can safely land without snagging. Still, for a long time I thought it would be a fine place to crawl up to a pool and drop a worm through the brush to a trout waiting beneath a fallen log. One afternoon in late May, following a long winter and a wet and stormy spring, I succumbed to the temptation. That is how I caught the King of Big Tesuque Creek.

I had been very busy at work. The weather had been lousy. I was stressed out and stir crazy, alternating periods of frenzied activity with long stretches of moping and staring at the snow-capped mountains behind the city. My mood was so foul that when I told my wife on a Sunday afternoon that I needed to get out of the house and hike for a few hours, she told me to spend the whole afternoon and suggested that I take a fishing rod.

I drove up the Ski Basin Road to the trailhead, parked and began walking down to the creek. The woods were lush from weeks of rain. On the way I met a family of overweight Texans struggling up the muddy trail. The father saw my fly rod and asked, "Are there any fish in that little stream?" I told him there were. He seemed shocked. "Do they stock it?" he asked. "No," I told him. "The creek hasn't been stocked for years." He looked skeptical but wished me luck. I continued on my way.

There is an intermittent trickle that follows the Bear Wallow trail down to Big Tesuque Creek. Two weeks of heavy afternoon rains had transformed the trickle into a small stream with pools deep enough to hold trout. I looked for fish but did not see any. It occurred to me that maybe the Texan had not gotten all the way to the creek and the "little stream" he had asked about was the trickle and not Big Tesuque Creek.

When I reached the creek, it was swollen with runoff and roaring. Two weeks earlier, my wife and I had crossed it without a thought, stepping from stone to stone. Not this time. The rocks that had risen above the surface a fortnight earlier were hidden beneath a foot of rushing water. I spent a few minutes searching for a safe way to reach the other bank, failed to find one and then crossed the creek on a slick spray-soaked tree trunk that lay across it. I counted myself lucky not to have fallen in.

After crossing the creek, I tied on a black wooly worm and began to fish up the stream. For a half-hour it was slow going. The water was moving very fast, the openings in the brush were small, and I hung the fly in the branches again and again. I did not see a single trout. Eventually, I succeeded in hooking a drowned log. That was the end of the wooly worm. I tied on a caddis larva. Minutes later, the dark form of a trout darted away from the bank beneath my feet into the shelter of a deadfall. I waited and then dropped the fly into a pocket of deep water next to the tangle of fallen timber where the trout had vanished. Nothing happened.

A hundred yards farther up the creek I saw a trout holding along a drowned tree trunk. I approached it carefully and dropped my fly into the current above the fish. The trout did not move. I waited and again drifted the nymph past the trout. After repeating this performance a half-dozen times, it dawned on me that the earth along the stream was moist and rich and that the trout was mine for the taking. I turned over a rock and found a fat worm. After replacing the rock, I hooked the worm on my nymph and lowered it into the stream above the trout. The trout raced for the worm, inhaled it and was on. Ten seconds later I held a nine-inch brown in my hand. It was my first trout of the season. I released the trout in the shallows on the edge of the stream. It held for a second, hovering above the pale gravel bottom. Then it darted into the torrent and was gone.

I saw a few more trout on my way up the stream, but they were in pockets so small or brush so impenetrable that I could not reach them without spooking them. It occurred to me that even though the trail was seldom more than a hundred feet away, I had not seen another person since I started following the creek up the mountain more than an hour earlier. The woods along the stream were thick and it was slow going through the thorny shrubs, brush and fallen trees. I decided to cut back to the trail and follow it to the meadow where it crossed the creek on a big tree trunk before winding back up the mountain to the trailhead. The creek was more open in the meadow. Perhaps it would be easier fishing.

I followed the trail up the hillside, through the meadow and down to the creek. The trunk of the big tree that spanned the stream had been worn smooth by the feet of countless hikers. I wondered how long the tree had lain there. It had been there when I first began taking Danny for walks eight years earlier. Above and below the fallen tree the creek was wide and open enough to cast a fly. I edged out onto the smooth trunk and cast the nymph upstream. I followed the leader as it drifted down in the swift current. Nothing happened. After a half-dozen casts my attention waned and my eyes were drawn to a pair of ravens high in the branches of a tree. As I picked up the line to cast again I felt resistance, saw the silver side of a trout and then the fish was gone. I continued to cast but nothing moved, so I crossed the creek and looked downstream.

At the end of the run, the creek deepened before spilling over a dam formed by fallen timber. The bottom was pale. I could see the darting forms of two small trout. And then, at the very tail of the run, I saw him. The King of Big Tesuque Creek. In the confines of the small stream, he looked huge. I turned over a flat rock near the bank. Beneath it I found only ants. I put it back in its place and tried another. This time I was rewarded with three worms. I eased the largest from its hole in the damp earth and hooked it on my fly. Then I cast the worm into the current above the big trout. I saw him move to the side and then felt a throbbing on the end of the line. I set the hook. The tiny fly rod bent double as the trout dashed for the drowned branches. I turned him and he raced up through the run, leapt clear of the water and then held in the current shaking his head. He made another short run but his strength was ebbing. A moment later I led him into the shallows where I freed the hook from his lip.

The trout was long and fat and sleek with deep yellow sides dotted with red. I admired him for a moment, trying to commit the picture to memory, before releasing him. Then I eased him back into the stream. He was very tired. I held him in the slow current along the bank until he regained his strength. For a moment he hung suspended in the shallows. Then with a flick of his tail he darted into the shelter of deep water beneath the tangle of drowned branches at the end of the run. Forty-five minutes later I was home too.

\* \* \*

Big Tesuque Creek is not a wild place, but the trout that live in it are wild fish. In a stream so close to a city of sixty thousand people, that is a remarkable thing. Trout and large numbers of human beings do not easily live in close proximity, and any stream that holds wild trout on the edge of a city is a special place. Big Tesuque Creek is more special than most. It is clean, free-flowing, and for the most part unspoiled.

If you asked me to put an economic value on the trout of Big Tesuque Creek, I would be hard pressed to do so. After all, what are trout worth in a stream where few people know they exist and fewer still fish for them? They do not generate jobs, draw tourists, or bring about any other economic activity that we can easily measure. But still they have value. Their value is in the richness of life they contribute to the world. Their value is that on a fall day, I can walk along the bank of the creek and, if I am watchful and quiet, I can see other lives played out in the clear water that tumbles down the mountain. It is a kind of wealth I hope my children's children will share. The value of the trout is, quite simply, that they exist.

# Chapter Eleven

## Beyond the Dark Tower

There is a mountain that rises like a dark tower keeping watch over the north slope of the Jemez Mountains. Behind the mountain there is a canyon. It is one of many that emanate like spokes of a wheel from the great mountain mass of the Jemez. A short trail leads down into the canyon. Reddish-brown pine needles blanket the earth and deaden my footfalls as I descend. Light filters down through towering ponderosa pines that grow along the steep hillsides and great Douglas firs that rise from the canyon floor. It is cathedral light, shafts of sunlight from high above softly illuminating the shaded floor of the canyon. Beneath the great trees are patches of oak with twisted limbs and dark green shiny leaves. Scattered stands of aspen dot the slope.

Near the bottom the sound of the creek rises up out of the canyon. It is the lilting musical sound of a small stream running gently across the forest floor. The creek runs at the base of the canyon beneath steep walls of basalt and volcanic tuff. It is a small creek, no more than a half-dozen feet wide in most places. Its waters come from melting snow, summer rains, and secret sources far beneath the earth.

The creek runs down into the Chama, which in its turn feeds the Rio Grande. It is one of dozens of tributaries that feed the big rivers like capillaries feed veins as they return water, the earth's blood, to the great heart of the sea in the Gulf of Mexico a thousand miles away. The creek is filled with fish. The fish are Rio Grande cutthroat trout.

\* \* \*

All the way to the creek the Dark Tower loomed in the background. Once seen, it was a mountain that you did not forget—steep, flat-topped, and almost black. According to the National Forest map, the creek was somewhere behind the mountain and drained its southern flank. On the map the creek had been a thin blue line. How thin I did not realize until the paved road crossed it near its entrance to a lake. It looked shallow, warm, and too small to hold any decent fish. I wondered if it would be worth the effort of reaching it.

The trip had begun in March with an idea, a list, and two maps. The idea was to find the perfect cutthroat stream. The list was a list of all the streams in New Mexico known to hold Rio Grande cutthroats. The maps were maps of the Carson and Santa Fe National Forests. I spent many evenings looking for the perfect stream. It needed to be remote but no more than a couple hours' drive from Santa Fe. It needed to be long enough to provide lots of fishing water, and it needed to be accessible by car but not paralleled by a road. One stream seemed to fill the bill. I had never heard anyone mention it. That was a good sign. My old *Guide to New Mexico Fishing Waters* described it as a "good little stream." That was another. I circled the stream on the map and waited for a free day. It came on a Sunday in early July.

After breakfast, I left Santa Fe and drove north and west past Española and Abiquiu until I came to a small village where I turned off onto a gravel forest road that headed up onto the north slope of the Jemez. Its washboard surface wound up into the mountains, climbing more than two thousand feet before leveling out in a narrow meadow fringed with ponderosa pines. As I entered the meadow, a bear, massive and brown, lumbered across the road. It was so large that if this had been grizzly country, I might have guessed it was a grizzly. But only black bears have lived in northern New Mexico since a rancher shot the last grizzly in the Pecos in 1923. The bear stopped and looked at the car. Then it dove into the brush on the edge of the meadow and disappeared.

The road skirted the north side of the dark tower and began to go up again. An unmarked side road turned off to the left. After stopping to check the National Forest map, I decided that it was probably the road I wanted. There was no way to be sure except to follow it. The side road was rough and deeply rutted. It had been a while since anyone had driven this way. Tall grass grew in the center of the road. I drove along a ridge and then zigzagged down the side of the mountain to a grassy shelf on the edge of a narrow, densely wooded canyon. On the map the road ended at the creek. In the real world it ended by a wooden fence in a small clearing surrounded by ponderosa pines.

I parked the car in the shade beneath the trees and walked to the edge. I was still far above the floor of the canyon. I could hear the sound of the wind in the trees but not the stream. I remembered how small it had been when I drove across it where it entered the lake many miles downstream. I hoped that it was still a live stream below me in the canyon and that it was not too warm for trout. The wind was hot. It was 10:30 in the morning.

A trail led down into the canyon. I took my rod, camera, and knapsack and followed it down through the forest. Fifteen minutes later I was at the stream. It was tiny and looked warm. In places brush and fallen timber choked the canyon floor. The air was cool. A slight breeze blew. Big cumulus clouds floated by high above the canyon walls. The little stream was alternately in light and shadow.

In a sunlit pool I saw the fish. Trout—tiny and not so tiny—finning in the dappled sunlight. I approached the pool and cast. As soon as the fly, a size 14 Adams, lighted on the surface, a trout rose. I set the hook . . . and missed the fish. On the next cast another trout rose. This time the hook held. Seconds later the fish was in my hand. It was a small perfectly formed Rio Grande cutthroat with crimson slashes beneath its gills, rose sides and black spots clustered near its tail.

For the next two hours I fished up the stream. Wherever there was a pocket or a pool more than a foot deep, trout rose and smacked the fly. All were Rio Grande cutthroats. Like the first, all were small but well-fed with deep bodies and small heads. They were healthy fish. The smallest were no more than four inches long. The largest, a ten-incher, exploded out of a deep, shaded pocket. This fish was different in appearance from the others. It was red-gold and covered with a thick slime. I wondered what the difference in appearance signified.

I caught fish after fish, but as usual, the big one got away. It was in a pool below a fallen tree, finning lazily and sipping an occasional insect from the surface. I could not tell what it was taking. There were a few light-colored caddis flies on the water and an abundance of mosquitoes and biting flies along the banks. I stalked the trout from below, waited, watched, and then cast. The fly landed short of the trout. The trout turned, swirled at the fly and then disappeared beneath the fallen tree. Later, on my way back downstream, I saw it again. I watched the fish as it fed, but I did not cast.

I said this fish was the "big one." How big was it? Perhaps eleven inches, maybe a foot, but these things are relative. A foot-long trout may not seem like much, but in the context of its surroundings it was a giant. This was a small stream. In places it was no more than four feet wide. The fish was fully a quarter of the stream's width in length. A trout of similar dimension in a large river like the San Juan would likely feed on anglers rather than insects.

Although the stream was very small, it had a gentle gradient and was well shaded. There were many places for trout to live and hide. I could cross it easily in my hiking boots to get the best casting angles. The trail that followed the stream was a good one, and it appeared lightly used. Still, there were occasional beer cans, bait containers, and empty packs of snelled hooks. I wondered what kind of an idiot would leave trash in a place like this.

I worked my way up the stream, catching trout after trout, releasing them and shooting nearly two rolls of film in the process. It was a day of light and shadow. Exposures changed constantly as clouds passed overhead. I could have fished until nightfall. But it was not to be. In the slice of sky above the canyon walls the clouds grew larger and darker. Some were almost black. In the distance thunder rolled. This was no place to be in a storm. The dirt road back up the mountain would turn to mush.

So I turned back. Still, my resolve to hike straight back to the car was shaken by several pockets and pools I had not noticed while fishing up the stream. The little creek was loaded, and more trout rose to the fly, an elk hair caddis that had replaced the Adams I had left in a tree limb on my way upstream. They were lovely fish, eight to nine inches in length, and they leapt clear of the water in the little runs. By the time I reached the trail that led back out of the canyon, I had half a mind to continue fishing downstream, to see what was there. Thunder rolled, and big drops of rain began splattering down through the trees. It was time to leave.

Driving down out of the high country I stopped the car and got out. Behind me the dark tower dominated the sky, framed in black clouds. Lightning flashed. Menace was in the air. The land before me was dry. But somewhere back down behind the mountain the little stream ran from pool to pool along the forest floor and the trout were waiting. I would be back.

* * *

Since I first discovered the creek several years ago, I have fished it many times. The trout are always there, quick to rise and very lovely. The trees along the narrow canyon floor stretch for the sky and shade the water. On summer afternoons, clouds gather and fill the slice of sky above the pale canyon walls. In the fall, aspen leaves float in the clear water. I am always alone. Lately, though, my pleasure has been tinged with sadness.

One spring morning I spent several hours with Mike Hatch at the Game and Fish Department. Mike is a leading authority on the fishes of New Mexico. In fact, he wrote the book on them. His book, *The Fishes of New Mexico* (1990), which he wrote with James and Mary Sublette, is a scholarly work that Mike once described to me as a good sedative for the general reader. It is definitely not a page-turner, but it does contain a wealth of detailed information about New Mexico, its waters, and its fish.

About once a year I give Mike a call, and we get together in his office, which is across the street from mine. We talk about fish and philosophy. I ask him questions and he answers them, sometimes in more detail than I can absorb. This time I wanted to show him some of the photographs I had taken of cutthroats from different streams and talk about the fish and their past, present, and future. When we met, Mike told me that the Department had recently done a study of Rio Grande cutthroats, and he offered me a copy. I read through it that evening after the boys had gone to bed.

There was a lot in the study that I already knew. But I learned some other things as well. The variation that I had noted between fish from different streams was not just the result of long-term adaptations to different natural environments. Instead, some of the differences were the result of human activities that had rendered the main streams unsuitable for cutthroats or impassable and thus prevented genetic interchange between fish in different streams. Dams, pollution, warm water, and exotic fish species all combined to isolate populations of cutthroats in headwater tributaries. Most of these tributaries were tiny and the populations of fish they could sustain were commensurately small. Isolation accelerated the pace of genetic differentiation. All this I knew.

But I had not pushed the idea of isolation far enough. Perhaps I had not wanted to. Divergence from other populations of Rio Grande cutthroats was one result of isolation, but there was another more ominous consequence. Over time, a small population of fish will become inbred unless new genes are periodically introduced into the pool. The consequences of inbreeding are known. A gradual decrease in the fitness of the population that potentially culminates in extinction. That was what was happening in my creek. The trout were genetically pure Rio Grande cutthroats, but they were also genetically uniform. They were already inbred. They still looked outwardly healthy, but there was a time-bomb ticking in their genes. Unless something happened, the isolation that protected them might in time kill them.

The solution to the problem is to introduce some genetic diversity into the creek. In the natural order of things, this was accomplished through migration, by fish moving from stream to stream. But the natural order of things no longer exists, and the channels of migration are not open. They are blocked by dams, pollution, dewatered streams and the presence of exotic fish species. Migration can be simulated by moving trout from one stream to another, which is what the Game and Fish Department study proposed, but it is not without risks.

At least some part of the variation between different populations of cutthroats is likely due to adaptation to different environments. If we add the wrong genes to the pool, we may create problems as bad or worse than those we are trying to solve in the form of fish ill-suited to the streams in which they find themselves. Experience with salmon in the Northwest and lake trout in the Great Lakes suggests that distinct strains of fish may be genetically attuned to micro-habitats. When they are stocked in strange waters, they may be incapable of reproduction in the new setting. Sometimes stocking works. Sometimes it doesn't.

In both New Mexico and southern Colorado there have been successful re-introductions of Rio Grande cutthroats into streams that they once inhabited, and the view among the people who ought to know is that Rio Grande cutthroats are adaptable enough so that fish from one stream will be able to survive and contribute genetic diversity in others. I hope they are right, because at least for now, it is probably the best we can do.

There is, of course, a straightforward approach to perpetuating the native trout of these mountains. Remove exotic trout from places where they don't belong. Stop stocking rainbow trout and let the rivers run where they will. Close the hatcheries. Get rid of dams and levees. Let grass and trees grow on the banks. Fat chance! There are faint rumors of this kind of thing happening in far off places, but in arid New Mexico, it is not about to happen any time soon.

Five hundred years ago, New Mexico was a greener place. Streams flowed deeper and cooler. Much of what is now desert was a grass-land, and the land was not scarred by arroyos. When the Spanish and other settlers came, they brought cattle and sheep. Over time the herds grew. Cattle trampled the riverbanks and stripped away the streamside vegetation. Sheep grazed the earth bare. Rivers spread and dried up. Arroyos formed. Logging scarred the mountains. When the spring runoff came, there was nothing to hold the water or the earth on the hillsides and sediment filled the rivers. There was no shade and the sun beat down on the water. Streams that once ran cool and deep all year suffered from siltation and extremes of temperature and flow. Cutthroat trout require cold clean water. The streams where they had evolved were no longer hospitable places.

It all hit rock bottom a hundred years ago. Most of New Mexico's big game had been exterminated, the herbivores by competition from cattle and sheep and the predators by systematic campaigns to eradicate them after their prey had disappeared and they turned to livestock as a source of food. The hillsides were bare, denuded for firewood and timber. Beginning in the 1890s, rainbow trout from the West Coast and brown trout from Europe were stocked in the degraded streams. At the time, it seemed like the thing to do. For the cutthroats, it was the kiss of death.

Rainbows interbreed with Rio Grande cutthroats and destroy their genetic integrity. Hatchery rainbows also compete with the native trout for food and space. Brown trout are more aggressive than the native cutthroats. They drive the natives from the best lies into marginal portions of the stream. They prey on the cutthroats' young. Browns are fall spawners while cutthroats spawn in the spring. All of these things conspire to give brown trout a competitive advantage over Rio Grande cutthroats. Put brown or rainbow trout in a cutthroat stream and the cutthroats disappear or their population declines sharply. The irony is that while browns and rainbows are perfectly capable of driving the native trout to extinction, they are, at least to my untrained eye, incapable of growing as plentiful or as large as Rio Grande cutthroats in New Mexico's marginal habitat.

Since the turn of the twentieth century, things have gotten better, albeit slowly. Much of the high country in which the rivers begin now lies within National Forests where there is a measure of control over grazing and logging and where there are mechanisms for environmental concerns to be aired. In the National Forests, the mountains look pristine and wild. It is an illusion. In many places the native plants are gone, replaced by exotic species. Even the roughest canyons have been logged. There is water in the streams, but they do not flow as strongly as they did five centuries ago. Once you leave the mountains, water becomes a commodity in which fish and wildlife have little say. From the Rio Costilla and Cimarron River in the north to the Rio Grande in the south, streams are regularly "de-watered," which means that all or nearly all of their water is diverted for human use leaving only empty streambeds. New Mexico is now the only state in the southern Rockies that does not have laws requiring minimum in-stream flows for the benefit of fish and wildlife. Many bills aimed at achieving that objective have been introduced in the state legislature. All have failed.

Today there is not much water, and the population is growing fast. Traditional agricultural uses of water compete with growing cities. Golf courses and glitzy developments sprout in the high desert. In rural areas, houses and trailers are appearing everywhere. State law confers the right to drill a well for domestic use and put in a septic tank on almost any piece of land that is three-quarters of an acre or larger. Water tables are falling. "It's our water. You can't have it." That's what they all say, from the acequias to Albuquerque. The voices are like a chorus of children shouting, "It's mine, mine, mine, . . ." Everyone has a claim to the water. There are more claims than water to go around. Everyone fears change. Everyone knows change is inevitable. Everyone is scared to budge an inch. We are frozen in an uneasy equilibrium. Free-flowing self-sustaining rivers are things of the past and perhaps the future. The streams in which Rio Grande cutthroats live are like islands in a hostile sea. For now, the trout will have to depend on us.

\* \* \*

The last time I fished the creek was a sad day. I had been working very hard and had just spent a week in court on a case that bore more than passing resemblance to Dickens's *Bleak House*. It was a fine warm day. The trout were brightly-colored and willing, but I needed more than the creek could give. Every fish I caught was a reminder. Even in the empty and tranquil canyon, a place where over the years I had seldom seen another human being, human activities were bringing about a slow and unconscious extinction. I longed for something wild and free. It was no longer there for me in the canyon.

Near the end of the day I held a trout in my hand. It was sleek and streamlined. Its colors were bright and alive. When I released it, the trout blended into the streambed and vanished in the shallow clear water. One moment it was there, fins quivering, hovering in the current. Then it was gone. Nothing is as it was. Change is the nature of things, but now we are the engine of change. We are both Noah and the Flood. Consciously or unconsciously, we hold the power of life and death. Many lives are in our hands. The fish was for me a symbol and embodiment of what the world has lost, what it still has to lose and what we can preserve, if we choose to do so.

It seems an easy choice, the choice between a world of streams inhabited by generic tame rainbow trout, incapable of sustaining themselves without human intervention, and a world of streams filled with a multiplicity of wild trout, each a mystery and a marvel. But the choice is less easy than it might seem. It is part of a conflict that is as old as ourselves, between two strains of human thought and endeavor. On the one hand we seek dominion over the earth. On the other we seek balance. Sometimes I think that the two are really parts of a whole, that they are different aspects of our drive to survive. Dominion aims at short-term prosperity and security. Balance takes the long view, that we cannot take more from the earth than we return to it. But there is more.

I find it hard to believe that any exotic trout would do as well in the creek as the native cutthroats. They have been there for millennia. Nature has fitted them for survival in what is at best a marginal habitat on the southern edge of trout country. They thrive and grow fat in a creek that is little more than a trickle. They fill its waters with beauty and life in a way that no brown trout or rainbow will ever be able to match. The Rio Grande cutthroat trout are of this place. They belong here like the basalt along the canyon floor and the ponderosa pines that reach for the sky.

But the importance of the Rio Grande cutthroat is at once more ephemeral and deeper. It is grounded in our ethics, values, and theology. It is grounded in a decent respect for all living things. It is grounded in the sense of mystery and wonder that is at the core of what makes us human. If creation is a great tapestry, the trout are one of its threads. They contribute color, richness, and integrity to the fabric of life. Pull out a thread, and the tapestry will remain, less vibrant than before but still intact. Pull out many threads and the tapestry will fade and eventually lie in tatters. If the trout in this tiny stream should ever cease to be, we will all be diminished, not just because the world will have become a poorer place, but because we had a choice.

# Chapter Twelve

## WINTER LIGHT

Several years ago while I was working on a short story about winter fly fishing, Mark at the fly shop jokingly suggested that I describe the Rio Grande as "a moody and humbling river." Just what is "a moody and humbling river," you ask. Well, what fishermen mean when they use those words is that the river is maddeningly unpredictable. Not inconsistent in the sense that fishing is tough at certain times of year or under certain weather conditions or anything rational like that. No, "a moody and humbling river" is a river that teems with trout one day and is fishless the next, even though water temperature, weather, and everything else I can think of except for the date on the calendar remains constant. It's enough to drive you crazy, and it's reason enough for lots of fishermen to avoid the Rio Grande like a plague even though the great river has big browns, wild cutbows, and spectacular scenery.

Winters are long in the mountains of northern New Mexico, and most trout streams are locked in snow and ice from the end of October until the runoff starts in spring. The Rio Grande is pretty much the only game in town. Strangely enough, in winter the Rio Grande is just a little less moody and humbling than it is at other seasons. At least that's what I start telling myself after the winter solstice when the days are just beginning to lengthen, I haven't fished in what seems like a lifetime, and tackle catalogues are starting to arrive in the mail.

On the Rio Grande, winter is the time of the snowflies. The term "snowfly" is generic. It refers to whatever type of midge happens to hatch in winter on the river you are fishing. The Rio Grande's snowflies are tiny midges with black bodies and gray wings. In winter

117

they hatch by the millions, sometimes blanketing the surface of the river. Sometimes. Nothing in fly fishing is ever a sure thing. That goes double for the Rio Grande.

I have read that on some streams snowfly hatches are best fished during the warmest part of the day and that precise imitations of the naturals are the most effective patterns. That may be true on some streams, but not on the Rio Grande. On the great river there are four keys to fishing the hatch. You should fish late in the day, from the time when the sun begins to set behind the walls of the Rio Grande Gorge until dark, or on overcast days. You should use cluster patterns rather than imitations of single midges. You should fish only to rising trout, and you should avoid fishing on very cold or windy days or when the water is very cold.

Like most rules, the ones I've just written were probably made to be broken. Sometimes. The Rio Grande is tough enough without doing things that lengthen the odds, and while on a lot of streams luck is enough to put you into fish, it seldom works that way on the Rio Grande. Besides, in winter only the truly daft want to be on the stream long enough to get lucky. If your time is limited or your sanity is even marginally intact and you want to catch fish instead of pneumonia, you play by the rules.

Some of them even make sense. On a winter day the trout begin to rise when the sun goes off the water. When they start to rise, blind casting is a good way to scare them silly, so you should cast only to rising trout. And when the water temperatures dip into the thirties, it is too cold for the snowflies and trout, and it should be too cold for you. But why cluster patterns work is a mystery. The conventional logic is that the snowflies are so small that the trout aren't interested in single insects. They will only rise to "clusters" of the tiny bugs. Well, I have watched trout rising to snowflies and I have seen plenty of them take individual insects. I have never seen a fish take a "cluster" of naturals, at least not one the size of a heavily hackled size fourteen dry fly. Be that as it may, until someone told me to use cluster patterns, I fished tiny, hard-to-see imitations of single flies and caught only the occasional tiddler. I have done much better using size fourteen and sixteen Griffiths Gnats, and they are much easier to see in the twilight than size twenty-two Midges with black bodies and gray wings.

The winter of 1992–1993 was cold and snowy. According to a report in the *Albuquerque Journal,* sixty percent of New Mexico's snow measuring stations reported the highest snow pack in history, and another twenty percent recorded the second highest. More than ten feet of snow fell at the ski basin behind Santa Fe. I did not fish from mid-October until a Sunday in late January. It was the first warm day in a long while. In Santa Fe the sun shone strongly, and the air was still. By noon the temperature had climbed into the mid-forties. We went to the mall and bought some clothes for the boys. When we left the mall in the early afternoon, I looked out across the parking lot to the snowy Sangre de Cristo range. I must have looked for a long time. My wife remarked that it was too nice a day to spend inside. I agreed. "Why don't you go fishing this afternoon," she suggested. "Well . . . o.k., if you insist." The car peeled out of the mall parking lot. Fifteen minutes later I had unloaded the boys' new jeans and sweatshirts, thrown my vest, waders, rod, down jacket, hat, and gloves in the back seat, gotten the dog and was driving north toward Pilar.

I drove fast, stopping only to pick up a cup of black coffee at the drive-through window of a fast food restaurant in Española. Forty minutes after leaving Santa Fe I reached the southern end of the Rio Grande Gorge at Velarde where the road descended to the river. The water was higher than it had been when I last fished the river in October, but it was not too high and the river was the clearest I had ever seen it.

The road followed the Rio Grande. Hills rose on either side of the river, pale sage green hills covered with chamisa, dotted with the hunched forms of piñons and junipers, and black basalt hills, with purple-brown boulders, dark and menacing. Far above, rough rubble fell away from high flat ridges. The southern flanks of the hills were bare, but the north slopes and shady places were covered with snow. In most places the hillsides ended at the water, but here and there the canyon floor opened a bit, and great old cottonwoods with thick trunks and twisted leafless limbs lined the bank. In gaps between the hills, the white forms of the Taos Range were visible in the distance. High feathery clouds floated across the sky.

At Pilar the road to Taos left the river and climbed up the mesa toward the town. I turned off and continued up along the river for several more miles until I came to the place I wanted to fish. I parked the car and looked at my watch. It was 4:00 p.m. It seemed a perfect winter day. The sun shone brightly. The river was clear and beautiful. But when I got out of the car the wind was blowing hard up the canyon against the current. In the pools the surface of the river rippled and grew dark from the squalls as they passed. Although the sun had not yet fallen behind the walls of the gorge, it was much colder than it had been in Santa Fe.

I let Cera out and she raced down to the river, took a long drink, and began patrolling the bank. I put on a heavy sweater, my neoprene waders, down jacket, watch cap, and vest. Then I rigged my rod. After tying on a size sixteen Griffiths Gnat, I walked down to the water. There were a few snowflies in the slack water that ran along the bankside boulders. I had expected to see more. The wind drove the tiny insects up against the current. It was not a good sign.

The sun sank lower, and I slowly walked downstream, scanning the water for flies and rising fish. I saw few flies and no fish. In the long flat pool where I had once seen dozens of trout rising on a sunny winter afternoon, nothing moved except the wind-driven surface of the river. As the sun sank behind the ridge, I reached the pool I planned to fish. The wind slowed. I worked my way down through the thicket of salt cedars that lined the bank until I came to a small opening near the tail of the pool where I could sit shielded from the wind and look out over the whole length of the pool. I pulled my cap down over my ears and watched the darkening water. Occasionally I could see the tiny forms of snowflies on the surface of the river, but the wind did not die and still no fish rose.

A hundred yards above me the great form of a heron lighted in the shallows by the far bank. I wondered what the bird was hunting. I had not seen a fish, not even a minnow, in the shallows as I made my way downstream. Ducks flew overhead, racing up the canyon with the wind at their backs.

Night was falling, and I sat on the bank among the salt cedars, waiting for the wind to die. And then, just as dusk faded into night, the wind stopped. I waited expectantly. Surely now the fish would begin to rise. But inside I knew that it would not happen. It was too late. If the rise had not already begun, tonight there would be no rise. The surface of the river was flat and unbroken. Then the wind started up again and it grew very cold. Darkness fell. I saw a few snowflies against the last light, but no trout rose. The river flowed, dark viscous water, almost metallic. Between black knife-edged ridges, the sky grew dark and filled with stars and a sliver of moon. Metallic water and clear sky. Black ridges. Stars. A sliver of moon. The sound of the river. The sound of the wind.

Beavers had been working the river, and I had seen fresh cuttings along the banks and a new dam on one of the side channels. As the last light faded, a beaver swam through the pool. I did not move, but the beaver sensed my presence, slapped a warning with its flat tail and dove beneath the surface. When the sound and the ripples faded, I pulled myself from my sheltered spot and walked up the river toward the car. Cera followed.

I started the car as soon as I reached it, hoping to warm up the motor while I was taking off my waders and putting away my gear. I opened the back and Cera jumped in and settled down. She seemed tired and happy to be out of the wind. My fingers were stiff from the cold, and it took forever to get out of the waders. Eventually, though, I succeeded in getting them off. When I put on my shoes they felt a size large on my cold-shrunken feet. Then I got in the car and began the trip home.

Just before I came to the main road I pulled over and got out of the car. There was a long slow pool here where I seldom failed to see rising trout in winter. I walked down to the river. The wind rippled the surface. I watched for several moments, but it was too dark to see and too cold to watch. I hurried back to the car and turned the heater on full blast.

I pulled onto the main road and headed south. In the east the sky was black, but the last light lingered on the western horizon. The hills were black and sharp against the glow. Just before the road veered away from the river, I passed under a huge dark bird flying along the road, following the river downstream. An eagle, I thought. I had seen them before on winter days, patrolling the river. It should have been a perfect ending, but I felt tired and just wanted to be home.

When I got home, Randy and the boys were not there. I got my things out of the car and fed Cera. Then I cooked a meal I had not eaten much since my bachelor days fifteen years earlier. Spaghetti mixed with melted cheddar cheese and tomato sauce. It was heavy, warm and filling, and it tasted very good.

Randy and the boys burst through the door just as I was finishing my meal. They had been to see a new Disney movie. Danny told me about it, talking so fast and throwing in so much detail that I couldn't follow it all. I made the boys a snack and then put Danny to bed. He was very excited, and he couldn't sleep. I asked him if he wanted me to read. "No, Daddy," he said. "Tell me another cave boy story." So I did. The "cave boy" was a prehistoric boy about Danny's age with a family much like our own that lived in a cave on the side of a hill overlooking a valley through which flowed a clear stream filled with trout.

In my story it was winter. Snow lay deep on the ground. On a brilliant blue day the boy and his father walked through the snowy woods along the creek. They came upon a set of tracks that the boy did not recognize. "What is it?" he asked. "A lynx," said his father. They followed the tracks along the stream. The tracks of the lynx crossed those of a snowshoe hare, recrossed and then followed them into the woods. The spaces between the footprints grew longer, and in a clearing in the woods, the tracks vanished in a jumble of wildly disturbed snow.

"What happened here?" the boy's father asked. "The lynx caught up with the hare," the boy said, "but he did not catch him." The boy's father was surprised. "How can you tell?" "Look, over there," said the boy. "Do you see where the tracks of the hare lead off into the woods? The tracks of the lynx do not follow. The lynx went the other way, off toward the stream." "You are a good tracker," said the boy's father, and together they followed the tracks of the lynx back to the frozen stream.

Danny's eyes were wide and dreamy. I went on with my story. That night the cave boy dreamed he was walking through snowy woods in the moonlight, following the tracks of a lynx. He moved silently through powdery snow. The snow reflected the moonlight and the shadows of the leafless trees made strange patterns on the snow. In a clearing in the woods he came upon the lynx. Their eyes met. They stood motionless in the moonlight. Then the lynx turned and vanished in the woods.

Danny's eyes were closed. He was breathing slowly and his head was warm and heavy against my shoulder. He smelled like he had when he was a baby. I got up slowly, kissed him on the cheek, and covered him with a blanket. I went to Adam's room. He was deep in a book. We talked for a few minutes before I said good night. Then I went and readied myself for bed. I was very tired.

After the boys were sleeping, Randy and I lay awake in bed. "Are you okay?" she asked. "I'm not sure," I answered. "Was it nice at the river?" she wanted to know. "Yes, it was beautiful, very beautiful, but I didn't see a fish, not even a minnow. Nothing." "But you always say that it doesn't matter if you catch fish," she said. Yes, she was right, that was what I always said, especially after catching two dozen wild trout on some mountain stream. I thought about it for a long time before the answer came to me. It should have been obvious. "I lied," I said. And with that we went to sleep.

# Bibliography

Barker, Elliott S. *Beatty's Cabin.* Albuquerque: University of New
  Mexico Press, 1953.

Behnke, Robert J. *Trout and Salmon of North America.* New York: Free
  Press, 2002.

Brown, David E. *The Grizzly in the Southwest: Documentary of an Extinction.*
  Norman: University of Oklahoma Press, 1985.

Chaney, E., Elmore, W. and W. S. Platts. *Livestock Grazing on Western
  Riparian Areas.* Washington, D.C.: U.S. Government Printing
  Office, 1990.

Cowley, David E. *Strategies for Development and Maintenance of a Hatchery
  Broodstock of Rio Grande Cutthroat Trout.* Santa Fe: New Mexico
  Department of Game and Fish, 1980.

Emory, William H. *Notes of a Military Reconnaissance,* reprinted in
  *Lieutenant Emory Reports.* Albuquerque: University of New Mexico
  Press, 1951.

Gould, Stephen J. *Eight Little Piggies: Reflections in Natural History.* New
  York and London: W.W. Norton and Company, 1993.

Leopold, Aldo. "The Deer Swath." *A Sand County Almanac with Essays
  on Conservation from Round River,* 223–24. New York: Oxford
  University Press, Inc., 1966; New York: Ballantine Books, 1991.

———. *Aldo Leopold's Wilderness.* D. Brown and N. Carmony, eds.
  Harrisburg, Pennsylvania: Stackpole Books, 1990.

———. *The River of the Mother of God and Other Essays.* S. Flader and J.
  Callicot, eds. Madison: University of Wisconsin Press, 1991.

Ligon, J. Stokely. *Wild Life of New Mexico: Its Conservation and Management.*
  Santa Fe: New Mexico Department of Game and Fish, 1927.

Martin, Craig, ed. *Fly Fishing in Northern New Mexico.* Albuqerque:
  University of New Mexico Press, 1991.

McClane, Albert J. *New Standard Fishing Encyclopedia,* 2nd Ed. New
  York: Holt, Rinehart and Winston, 1974.

Murray, John A., ed. *The Great Bear: Contemporary Writings on the Grizzly.* Anchorage and Seattle: Alaska Northwest Books, 1992.

Murray, J. A. *The South San Juan Wilderness Area: A Hiking and Field Guide.* Boulder, Colorado: Pruett Publishing Company, 1989.

New Mexico Department of Game and Fish. *Operation Plan.* Santa Fe, 1987.

———. *Handbook of Species Endangered in New Mexico.* Santa Fe, 1988.

———. *Long Range Plan for the Management of Rio Grande Cutthroat Trout in New Mexico.* Santa Fe, 2002.

Peacock, Douglas. *Grizzly Years: In Search of the American Wilderness.* New York: Henry Holt and Company, 1990.

Pettitt, Roland A. *Exploring the Jemez Country.* Los Alamos, N.M.: Pajarito Publications, 1975.

Quammen, David. *The Song of the Dodo.* New York: Scribner, 1996.

Santa Fe Group of the Sierra Club. *Day Hikes in the Santa Fe Area* (3rd Ed.). Santa Fe: Santa Fe Group of the Sierra Club, New Mexico, 1990.

Smith, Robert H. *Native Trout of North America.* Portland, Or.: Frank Amato Publications, Inc., 1994.

Sublette, James E., Mary Sublette, and Michael D. Hatch, M.D. *The Fishes of New Mexico.* Albuquerque: University of New Mexico Press, 1990.

Sutherland, Patrick K. and Arthur Montgomery. *Trail Guide to the Geology of the Upper Pecos.* Socorro: New Mexico Bureau of Mines and Mineral Resources, 1975.

Trotter, Patrick C. *Cutthroat: Native Trout of the American West.* Boulder: Colorado Associated University Press, Boulder, 1987.

U.S. Fish and Wildlife Service. *Candidate Status Review for Rio Grande Cutthroat Trout.* Federal Register: June 11, 2002 (Volume 67, Number 112).

Wilson, Edward O. *The Diversity of Life.* Cambridge, Mass.: Belknap Press of Harvard University Press, 1992.